Mark Bravo knows at an innat[...]
go the distance. As his book [...]
everything he has to everything he does—whether it be running,
living, or loving. His book is a how-to guide on how to find your
very own 'staying power,' and as Mark shows us, it has everything to do with a joyful, can-do attitude which eventually takes
you to the ultimate goal in life...finding your best self.

—TRACY BRYAN
Director of Public Relations, Golden State Donor Services

Through this book, Mark taught me a key thing about life...you
can still get to your destination even when you vary your pace to
take in the world and meet the people along the way.

—CHARLES HOWELL
Associate Chief Learning Officer, Writer, Philosopher

Momentum is a great book to use for daily inspiration each
morning. Mark's encouraging advice and wisdom starts my day
off in a positive way. Coach Bravo's book will hit home for athletes of all abilities.

— AMY DOWNS
President/CEO-Allegiance Credit Union,
Survivor of Alfred P. Murrah Federal Building Bombing,
Ironman Finisher

Like most people, I've had some setbacks on the road to achieving my goals. Coach Bravo's book has not only been a map leading me back to where I left off, but also a reminder that the best
time to start—or start again—is now. *Momentum* is an invalu-
able tool for anyone in pursuit of a high-quality life.

—MARISSA HENNIGAN
National Writer, Content Producer, and Athlete

77 OBSERVATIONS TOWARD A LIFE WELL LIVED

MARK BRAVO

Momentum

Mark Bravo will always try to accommodate speaking to a group, or appearing for a book signing or an interview. For more information or to book an appearance, contact Mark Bravo at:
runbravo@yahoo.com
or by phone at: (405) 824-8385

To order autographed copies online:
www.oklahomabooksonline.com/momentum

ISBN 978-1-63302-094-8
ISBN (eBook) 978-1-63302-095-5

This edition printed in 2018.

Publishing and Printing
by Total Publishing and Media (Tulsa, Okla.)

"Our deepest fear is not that we are inadequate. Our deepest fear is that we are powerful beyond measure. It is our light, not our darkness, that most frightens us. We ask ourselves, 'Who am I to be brilliant, gorgeous, talented and fabulous?' Actually, who are you not to be? You are a child of God. Your playing small doesn't serve the world. There's nothing enlightened about shrinking so that other people won't feel insecure around you. We were born to manifest the glory of God that is within us. And as we let our own light shine, we unconsciously give other people permission to do the same. As we are liberated from our own fear, our presence automatically liberates others."

—NELSON MANDELA

DEDICATION

It happens in a million different ways, and often unbeknownst at that moment to the giver, or receiver. I call it impact. I speak from experience here, having been touched on a grand scale by many people throughout my nearly 60 years, a number of whom are mentioned in the coming pages.

We are conditioned to think that the growing that goes on in life is reserved for the young. If so, then what I've been telling my friends for some time has newfound validity; I'm fifteen years late for everything! Whether youth is indeed wasted on the young, Yogi Berra had it right, when he infamously proclaimed: "It ain't over 'til it's over." One never knows when a new path will arise, previously unanticipated, or when your passion will take over. At that precise moment, though, the way you perceive life, and the canvas of what you hope to offer the world begins to form its artwork.

To all my athletes, who continue to raise my game. I hope I've lent as much to yours. Elite weekend warriors, and those who never dreamed they'd cover one mile. You all continue to encourage me by your spirit, fortitude, and stick-to-itiveness. You teach this coach a lot, foremost that you can always take another step. You were instrumental in my penning this book.

To contributors to this book, who either by their actions, examples, or writings have helped form its evolution. And to my "band of brothers," the tight-knit group of buddies from the dormitory years at Oklahoma University. To say I'm proud of our nearly 40-year friendship is a massive understatement. Long live Jordan House!

To my family: to a person one couldn't find more encouragement, not only in pursuing this book, but throughout my whole life. My three sisters, Joan, Jan, and Vikki, who had to endure their little brother having his own bedroom when they didn't. To Joan, and her husband, Mike, the first book authors in the family. May you continue changing the world with your Respect Diversity Foundation. Your twins: Michelle, I'm so proud of you for your quiet, gentle way of adding to the world around you, and Josh, who hits home runs for us all every day. As much as anyone, you're a template to a "life well-lived."

To Jan, the first doctor in the family (don't worry; I won't be the second). May you forever feel as deeply about what you believe in as now, and your heart of gold always be nurtured. Thanks for watching all the games with me; may there be many more. And Vikki, the angel of the family, who does for others as it would be drawn up in an instruction manual, with no concern for what comes back to her. Unassuming, Vikki upholds unique standards. Her 90/10 rule means 90 percent of what she does is for others, and maybe 10 percent for herself. I long ago realized I could try forever to emulate you and never get there. Always know, though, that the lesson is learned. And Gerry, my brother-in-law, who has added so much to our family. I anxiously await our next in-depth conversation. Better siblings than you I can't imagine.

To my Uncle Joe, who lived life on his own terms. There were tribulations at times, but nothing made him waver from living it, like the Chairman of the Board, Frank Sinatra, who looked a lot like him, "his way!"

To my Father, of whom you'll read in the coming pages; I hope you're aware of your greatest lesson to me: Showing the way, not talking about it. You made being a Bravo mean a great deal to me, and I try always to uphold that standard in a way that would make you quietly smile, as you always did when I knew something had meaning to you. We miss you greatly.

And my mother. Ruth Bravo's presence is felt wherever she goes, and like most of the great ones, she doesn't even know it. As the one "out front" as a parent, you showed me what unwavering love for family really means, and never more so than in

Dad's last years. I'm so grateful the three of us worked together so long, and that you gave me the "easy payment plan" when you won the majority of our football bets, which was always the case. Thank you for always encouraging me, and when things didn't go well, never reprimanding, only guiding. I love you and miss you very much.

And finally, to the one who occupies a spot no one else has: Leslie. No "We've only just begun" renditions, as I feel I've known you most of my life. You married a fifty-one-year-old kid, and on that day gave him the honor of entering a family that includes your five boys and eleven grandchildren (and counting). You're breathtaking, and everyone sees that, but it's not what brought us here: you touch my heart in ways no one ever has. The dozen-year journey we took that led to our wedding under the chuppah had as many "valleys" as "peaks," and for that I'm grateful. In a way, my life began when I told you how I saw our lives playing out (we weren't even dating). The change came when you actually listened. I'll try always to make you happy you made that call!

Leslie, I'll always run, and I'll always write. Thank you for encouraging me to do both.

To all who open these pages, I wish for you a few worthy observations to keep forever. As well, may you enjoy a lifelong pursuit—for that's what it is—of what makes you happy, and the ability to see not only what is right in front of you, but what lies beyond. Have a truly *"world-class"* life, athletes!

TABLE OF CONTENTS

Foreword   17
Introduction   21

PART ONE: Timing   23

Momentum   25
Understatedness   31
Athlete   37
Reach   41
Making Your Mark   47
Optimism   49
Peace   53
Intangibles   57
Gratitude   61
All Encompassing   63
Gratitude First...and Always   67
Balance   71
Team   73
The Necessity of Change   75
Impact   79
Repairing the World   83
Timing   87
Now   93
Self-Discipline   97
Seasons   101
Strive   105
Storms   109
Tests   111
Luck: When You're Primed, It Finds You   115
Surrender   117
You Win   119

PART TWO: Character   121

Flow   123
Fear or Fear Not?   127
Selflessness   131
Where To?   133
Beginnings   135
Serenity   139
Move Forward   145
Architect Your Character   147
Evolve   149
Humility: Negative to Positives   153
Possibilities   157
Victory   161
Self-confidence   163
Believe   165
Tranquility   169
Good Enough   171
Practice   175
Perfect Practice   177
Patterns   179
Nimble   183
Focus   185
Vision   187
Calibrate Higher   191
Are You Kidding Me?   193

PART THREE: Ol' Mo   195

Olympic   197
Strive   201
Aspire   203
What Have You Got?   207
Competing: Who's Really the Opposition?   211
Ordinary Miracles   215
Progress   219
Aspire—But to *What?*   223
Play   225
Integrity   229
Care Deeply or Don't Bother   231
Looking for Ol' "Mo"   233
Flow   235
Prosperity   237
Thrive   239
Carpe Diem   241
Release   243
Time   245
The Road to Peace of Mind   247
Peace of Mind   251
Your Best Version of You   253
Reputation   255
Stuck   259
Virtue   263
Giving Back   267
All You Want   271
Live Well Lived   273

ADDENDUM: Ordinary Heroes   278

FOREWORD

One of the key lessons you learn quickly in whitewater kayaking is the value of momentum. As you sit in your seven-foot enclosed kayak at the top of a challenging rapid evaluating what stands between you and the calm water below, you quickly discover that you have choices. Over the roar of the rapid, you intuitively "read" the water as it rushes downstream, deflecting off boulders, and falling over ledges. You literally might have hundreds of options in a single rapid. Your objective is to choose a path through the rapid that harnesses and transfers the energy of the charging water into your kayaking style and strategy.

If you succeed, your body balance, boat position and timing of critical strokes lead to an effortless navigation of the rapid. It's almost as if the water did all of the work for you.

But what if something goes a little wrong? A breaking wave sideswipes your kayak four feet in the wrong direction, perhaps turns you around backward, or even worse capsizes your boat upside down. Such situations can feel more like a struggle with the water. You're no longer on your "Plan A" and it's not football or basketball—you can't call "time-out" or take a break in the action! You have to re-invent your plan and do this on the fly. You have to create new momentum.

Fixing a mistake effectively is as critical a skill as getting something correct in the first place. Both effortless and challenging situations provide lessons in momentum, and while each is completely unique, both can be immensely rewarding.

Since winning America's first ever Olympic Gold Medal in Whitewater Canoeing at the 1992 Olympic Games, I reflect often about the life lessons I've learned from the river and none more than the value of momentum. Momentum is not an accidental occurrence. It's an equation of unique variables relative to your own goals and values. Define your variables, maximize each one of them, add them together and you have your formula for momentum.

One formula for momentum I've become a huge fan of is that of Mark Bravo. I've come to know Mark and wife, Leslie, during my frequent visits to Oklahoma City developing the sport of canoe/kayak in this amazing city. Mark possesses a rare type of happiness found in people today—a happiness driven by life's simple pleasures, a healthy curiosity about what motivates people, a perceptive view of the landscape around his community, and fresh perspective on power of growth and change.

Mark's passion for running, affinity for sports, and love for family are the roots for *Momentum: 77 Observations Toward a Life Well-Lived*. The life lessons you take away are not the latest trends and have no expiration date. Just proven, time-tested values that we so often overlook when we lose focus on what's important.

One of my sports psychologists' favorite mantras is, "It's not about what happens. It's about choosing your response to what happens." When it comes to finding, creating and sustaining momentum, we have the ultimate power of choice. We choose our frame of mind from the moment we wake up. We choose our reactions to all communications streams, and we choose the way we fuel ourselves for success—physically, emotionally and spiritually. Mark exemplifies these ideals on a daily basis and the results are simple—he becomes momentum's master. You can re-position yourself to do the same.

On the road to living better, improving relationships, being happier, and giving back, today you chose to read this book. In your own navigation of the river that is life, you consciously chose to discover, increase, and sustain momentum. By any definition, that is a good day on the river.

— JOE JACOBI

Spring 2010

A two-time Olympian, Joe Jacobi won America's first-ever Olympic Gold Medal in Whitewater Canoe Slalom in 1992.

INTRODUCTION

How you measure success is up to you. Whether it's the money you accumulate, the recognition in your community, or fame you generate, there are key elements involved that are necessary to truly feel this elusive reward.

Why is one person successful when another who is given to similar opportunity or talent fails? Why does one with unimaginable wealth sometimes emit such discontent, while serenity clearly seem abundant with another of much lesser means?

How do you "elevate" your existence to the next level, so that you create what you regard as a *life well lived?*

The answer to those questions is simple and threefold: *character, compassion,* and *peace of mind.* When you achieve the first two, the third follows. It's the journey that takes courage, patience, and a leap of faith.

The corridor to these answers, I feel, lies in the upcoming pages, and my hope is you'll benefit greatly from that passageway.

Within the pages of this book lay a series of points that I believe will keep you on a path to a life well lived. Your first level of success will begin by simply taking the journey.

My goal is to act as a compass, to help you arrive, and to keep you on the path toward being the best you can be. After all, what more can we ask of anyone, or ourselves?

PART ONE

TIMING

"To give less than your *best* is to sacrifice the *gift*."
— STEVE PREFONTAINE

1

MOMENTUM

Sometimes the circumstances in our lives leave us with few choices, and yet there is always one powerful choice left. It is the freedom to choose our own response to anything that happens to us—to choose our own attitude and reaction. A conscious *awareness* of this, either at that pivotal moment or at some point in the process, *allows* you to sculpt your makeup. You can live in fear of making a move or let your approach to adversity define you, sometimes for the rest of your life.

In 2005, my running having largely been unaffected by intrusions such as injury, I began feeling tightness, discomfort, and intermittent pain in my left hip periodically while on the roads. When it became pervasive—present almost every run—I consulted with a running doctor who's seen everything in his thirty-five years of treating runners. He's a great friend, Dr. Tom Coniglione, so I knew he'd get to the heart of the matter as quickly as possible. The second time I visited, with no improvement, it was x-ray time. When the doc returned, his first words were, "First thing you need to decide is if you want to continue to be a runner!"

While an optimist through and through, when faced with adversity, I create an exercise where I visit mentally a "worst-case" scenario, so I can quickly realize that even that is survivable. I landed on a possible stress fracture. While never having sustained a broken bone, many runners experience this, and I'd get through it, let it heal, and come back strong. You might imagine the shock when he said those words to me. When I assured him he knew what the answer was, he proceeded to lay out my options. The inevitable outcome? A hip replacement.

I believe numbness, maybe with a bit of *shock* sprinkled in, is the best way to describe my feelings the rest of that day. As an athlete who considered himself, as many athletes do, largely bulletproof and a never-say-die *optimist*, I took the best-case scenario from every option presented to me over the coming weeks.

When the dust settled, I chose to have a hip arthroscopy, in hopes of circumventing a total hip replacement. The doctor did his best and even said, "This could buy you a year or six years—you never know!" Naturally, never having been threatened with a career-ending injury, I wasn't even allowing that sort of negativism to creep into my psyche. I thought to myself, *Okay, I'll get twenty years and decide from there!*

About a year later, I began looking for the next step to take. Notwithstanding the fact I was trying everything to feel "normal" (full-fledged rehab without overdoing it), it was clear I needed to keep pursuing the right approach to getting what I considered my physical independence back. The doctor had done all he could; I simply hadn't found the answer yet.

What I feared was coming to pass; I needed a total hip replacement. I wasn't worried about the surgery. What scenario came after that weighed on my mind. Would I still be an athlete? (This time frame is what really formed my opinion of what the word *athlete* entails!) More specifically, would I run? Neither of these I doubted; I wouldn't let myself. It wasn't easy though. I had always said to my athletes that if I were ever unable to run, I'd find a way to be active. Low and behold, at age forty-eight, darned if I didn't have to walk the talk!

I did my homework before choosing a doctor. However, let me explain what that meant—I researched how feasible it was for me to continue running after the procedure, as most doctors espouse, when asked: "Running? Game over!"

I spoke to a few people who were running post-hip replacement and asked every type question. A very good friend of mine, whom I proceeded to coach, is sixty-five years old and even doing "ultra" events, which span more than a marathon in distance. My goals were different though. I wanted to run in a similar fashion that I had prior to this condition. Of course my speed wouldn't be the same, but I wanted to run with the same "verve," the goal being to run as smoothly as if I had never had an issue. It would take very specific range-of-motion work and diligent rehabilitation to redevelop the muscles severed during surgery, in addition to taming the ego in taking all the precautions put before me after surgery. Maybe above all else, patience would be required in not overdoing things, thus continually setting myself back, if not undoing the surgery completely.

I spoke to one highly recommended doctor who was very experienced in joint replacement. It was clear from the start we weren't on the same wavelength. His comment was, "You're going to have to alter your perception of exercise." While I knew this and was slowly coming around to buying in, I didn't agree with the level at which he thought I needed to change things. It made perfect sense, but this was one of those moments I implemented the thought processes that follow in this book. In some instances, with careful thought and solid doses of reality interspersed, the intangibles we tap define what we make of our lives.

Keep in mind I respect those doctors who say you shouldn't run. I also totally understand those runners who have this surgery and choose not to return to the sport.

I believe with all my heart, though, that we're all different, and we have the ability to rise above roadblocks that seem impenetrable. We possess, or can develop, characteristics in certain areas that allow us to raise our game and beat the odds. This doesn't mean the doubts, fears, and even setbacks that are prerequisite to such a battle become extinct. They still appear.

The intangible, though, as I saw it, was simply this: I was born to run, and it was going to happen.

Through a trusted cohort mentioned above who had the procedure and Dr. Coniglione, who is literally and figuratively a running doctor, I chose to see Dr. Tom Tkach to perform my surgery. Dr. Tkach is renowned around the country as a hip surgeon, and he happens to practice in my hometown of Oklahoma

City, Oklahoma. It was clear early on that we were a good match—like-minded in that he respected my desire to be extra-active post surgery. Taking my age and conditioning into consideration, he saw no reason I couldn't pursue running.

The singular negative comment that I heard from Dr. Tkach happened to be the first words he uttered upon our meeting. He had my MRI and X-rays already, and he greeted me with a handshake and proclamation that at some point I'd need something done to the other hip.

Being already overwhelmed a bit by the prospect of this first surgery, I steeled myself to a mentality of "cross that bridge when you confront it." While my optimism is usually brimming, the notion of one negative spoken by a professional (especially concerning your general health) can overtake the hundreds of positives you receive from the same person.

I used my two-year checkup in 2009 to broach the subject of my right hip, reminding him of what he had said before my left hip procedure. As Tkach spoke praises about how the X-rays looked, he replied, "I don't see you having a problem with it. It's not a normal hip, but it's fine!" The glass is three-quarters full, not half-empty. Case closed…for now anyway.

Indeed, it's been a process battling that mind-set of "what if's," and when particularly trying, I re-examine one of my favorite quotes.

> The *fear* won't help you save what you have; it
> will make you lose what you could become.

Every time you battle that uncertainty or hesitation, ultimately that inevitable *fear*, you strive to better yourself and test limits. You take something from the lesson, and it's with you always…for later implementation.

I had a surprisingly smooth recovery and return to running. A ten-miler with renowned marathoner Dick Beardsley in December 2007 (seven months after surgery) convinced me I was back, and it's been smooth sailing since. I'm reminded on the roads now and then that prudence is still in order, and I have adjusted certain goals (mostly speedwise). Also, I realized I can be very content without running another marathon. This feels unlike compromise to me but more like maturity. If we're blessed with a bit of wisdom, we all have acceptable boundaries we're willing to draw. All the time we must keep gratification and accomplishment key in the equation toward a life of quality and upping the calibration of the world.

I say now unequivocally that whatever my hip "journey" took temporarily from me in terms of independence and permanently in number of miles I choose to run, it's given me multiples back. You ask how this is possible after such a three-year roller coaster of uncertainty blended with disappointment. I identify it as adopting a "kinder, gentler" approach to life in general, one of optimism, using adversity to "put your signature on the project"!

Go get 'em: Life gets tough and the path uncertain for everyone:

1) Realize you will survive.
2) Realize you will grow from it.
3) Take one step forward; breathe, think, unleash the survivor inside.

"Intangibles can't be touched or felt. They come first and foremost from the desire not to settle for what is widely considered good enough."
— MARK BRAVO

2

UNDERSTATEDNESS

I have been an athlete all of my life. As a young boy, I was always outside playing some kind of sport. I guess you could say that being an athlete and playing sports are in my blood. Running, football, basketball—you name it; I played it. Sports defined me.

Many true athletes are good at almost any sport they play. Take my longtime friend John Allen. I have known John for years, and he never ceases to remind me that true talent often lies in people who are monumentally understated. John can play any sport. Anything. However, his talents don't stop there. He is musically inclined, he is a voracious reader, and he is a quick learner. John takes every opportunity as a challenge, whether it is studying Czechoslovakian poets, reading Shakespeare, or running a marathon. He's a talented, extremely well-rounded individual—a true Renaissance man. Yet his greatest trait? Understatedness.

It may seem to many that John is a natural athlete. While that is true, it only reflects a partial image of John. He is athletically inclined, no doubt. Yet there are many natural athletes who end up out of shape with no momentum in life. What makes John different?

That's easy. Tenacity. Tenacity starts with a single moment of faith. It is that moment that begins the journey, that starts building momentum, that perseveres when others become distracted.

My buddy John has the ability to leave the clutter in his life behind and move forward toward the destination. He understands momentum, and he knows that momentum starts with that first moment of decision followed by the actions necessary to persevere.

"There is no teaching to compare with example."
-SIR BADEN POWELL

My father was like that. My father had a drive to build a business, and he had the faith that if he stuck with it, no matter what setbacks occurred, everything would arrive at a successful and desirable outcome.

Our family business was a pawnshop. I've noticed lately much interest in the pawn business, and I even saw a reality television show based on the pawn industry. While it is entertaining to many, it was a lifestyle to us, and it was somewhat different than television portrays.

I learned something from all of those years working there with my dad and my mom. It takes teamwork to make anything successful. My dad loved us kids, and even better, he liked us! He really did! I realized, as the years passed, that my dad and mom had a team that was unshakable. If my dad only had my mom, he would have been fine, though he was consummately, albeit quietly, so proud of all four of his children. He cherished my mother. Together they were unstoppable, and together they created a firm foundation and good home for us while establishing a flourishing business in an environment that had the potential to bring people into our lives from all walks of life.

In later years I realized that my dad's "unspoken" example taught me another most valuable lesson: positive habits become a "way of life." He worked long hours, for years as long as twelve- to fourteen-hour days, but one thing daily was nonnegotiable—a trip to the YMCA. By his actions, not verbal commandments, his steadfast attention to physical fitness was the forbearer of my passion for running and overall health.

When I was five, I vividly remember doing pushups—on my father's back as he did his own pushup regimen! Now over forty-five years later I take a single action daily, my way of being closer to "the best I can be." That self-empowering act is almost always pushups, an act started with my father long ago.

There are all kinds of teams, and I am sure you never heard of my most gratifying team. Emmanuel Synagogue had a high school basketball league, and I am still proud today to consider myself part of that team that formed so many years ago. We played church league basketball, and I must tell you that although I enjoyed basketball, I do not have the stature of a typical basketball player. I'm not sure many of us back then fit the mold. We were just a bunch of Jewish guys who were ill equipped to play together—but we were a team.

As it turns out, we had a winless season. Oh, I think there might have been one win due to a technicality, maybe a forfeit, but we didn't honestly win one game that year. So what made it so gratifying? It was all about the journey that we embarked on together. When we lost, we got up and practiced one more time. We kept moving forward, never stopping. There was success because we never quit. Our "win" was found in finishing the season together, sticking together, moving forward together.

It is easy to be an armchair quarterback and second-guess a coach or a player. It is easy to blame someone else when you find yourself on a losing team. Yet one thing I discovered from that team was that I was responsible for what I did as part of the team. I was responsible for that three-point shot that I put up but didn't go in. I was responsible for letting the coach know when I needed his help. As part of the team, I am responsible for my own actions, my own attitude, and my own behavior.

Part of accepting that responsibility is finding a mentor to help you train, to keep you on track, to advise you to rethink a choice, and most of all to encourage you. My father had my mother to stand by his side, to encourage him. She was the face and voice of our business all of those years as my father did his part, working hard and being consistent. In turn, my father was my mentor. He lived his life in a way that taught me by example.

Now I have had the honor to mentor many others during my lifetime, and it is one of the true rewards this life gives me. I often learn as much from the person I mentor as he or she learns from me, and not surprisingly, the blessing ends up flowing both ways.

Yet in that beginning moment, when the shoes get laced up for the first time, when the sun is rising, and the dew is still on the morning grass, it's in that magical moment that my heart soars with sheer joy. The joy comes from gratitude for being able to do what I'm about to do, whatever it is. I know the momentum has begun. The first step in the journey can never be undone. With awareness and grace, one has agreed to leave sight of the shoreline and go to the deeper things in life, the oceans of life, for in the deep is where treasures are found.

Go get 'em: Wake up your ability! It's inside; have the courage to let it emerge!

"Do what you can, the best you can, from where you are."

3 ATHLETE

Are you an *athlete*?

When you hear the term *athlete*, what comes to mind? Adept at running, jumping—the *physical* I would imagine. I approach this powerful word altogether differently, though. Sure, athletes come in every physiological demographic; they can be graceful, powerful, fast, and built like gazelles. That's the easy definition.

My friends, clients, fellow runners, and everybody who's spent any time with me knows I place *immense* value on the term *athlete*. What I'm about to share is how I define the word and why it transcends physical accomplishment.

As mentioned, I've always been active—an athlete by traditional terms. While not exceptional, I held my own pursuing my younger years' passion of basketball. This translated to an innate running ability I've been fortunate to enjoy some three decades and still do. By some, I'm considered an athlete, and that always brings a certain level of gratification and gratitude.

The difference in how I view the term and its application is simple. When I label one an *athlete*, it speaks more to the whole person. One's intestinal fortitude, staying power, and grace under pressure mean every bit as much as their 5K time in a race. For me, the embodiment of a true *athlete* is clear-cut: one doing the very best they can under particular circumstances, especially those in which adversity plays a part. When we're backed against the wall, only then can we truly show others, and ourselves more importantly, what we're made of.

Take one of my dearest friends, Kayna, whom I've known twenty years and for whom I always held the utmost respect.

Nearly that entire time, she'd tell you I've referred to her as *athlete*; and as with many, early on she was puzzled with my use of the term for her. We met twenty years ago, at the height of my running career (if speed is your barometer, anyway). Our passions were very different. While it was very evident then the focus I placed on my sport and that her interests were seemingly diametrically opposed, our friendship and mutual respect grew.

Applying the term *athlete* to Kayna had nothing to do with her athletic prowess. Kayna had just undergone serious back surgery when we met, and the letter she wrote a friend (in the following chapter) will show you how far one can go in life with intestinal fortitude, stick-to-itiveness, and belief in one's self. Also, another very important lesson in life emerges: count nothing out! The unexpected turns, which are inevitable in life, can and often do serve as our "jump start" to new horizons that we don't think possible or haven't even imagined yet!

Go get 'em: What kind of athlete are you? Go to your strength, and *run with it!*

"There's an *athlete* inside each of us waiting to be released."

4

REACH

Kayna wrote the entry below to a friend of hers, who couldn't come to terms with a breakup after years of marriage and the effect it would soon have on her. It encompasses the *athlete* inside better than any description of mine.

On Sunday, September 9, 2001, I was lying on my hammock in the backyard. I'd just finished a lovely brunch at Pearls with some very good friends. I rocked on the hammock on a perfect autumn day with a bit of a fading champagne buzz, checking off the list of things I was grateful for. My family was happy and healthy and close; I finally owned a house in a neighborhood I'd wanted to live in for many years; I had a job that I adored; I worked with a doc who was among my best friends; the list went on and on; and I was brought to tears for my good fortune, and I gave thanks for it. Within forty-eight hours, the twin towers were rubble and the world was forever changed. It's likely you and I watched those towers fall together. Within six weeks the job that I thought I'd have forever was also forever changed. My professional position was gone, as was the man who was my friend. The story continues spiraling down from there: my perfect life was gone. Suddenly, unexpectedly gone. Maybe through no fault of my own. I spent the next three years in a emotional free fall, coming as close to rock bottom as I ever have. Those three years were some of the worst of my life, and I am profoundly thankful for them.

But for the darkness of my soul those years I wouldn't have the life that I have now. A new "perfect life," a better life. I was given an opportunity to re-invent myself yet again. I wonder if that day on the hammock, my prayer of gratitude wasn't just a spark for the divine to know it was time for me to move on. Everything I needed to know right then, I had learned. So, time to shake things up yet again and present me with the opportunity to grow. After my back surgery for scoliosis in 1990, I had restricted myself on physical activity. I'd tried in 1992 to begin running, I wanted to surprise my friends Mark and John, whom I had met *just after* back surgery, by running the Redbud Classic 5K in Oklahoma City that spring. For years I'd been there at the finish line to cheer them on. I wanted to run it with them and to surprise them by doing so. Unfortunately sciatic pain from training sidelined that, and I thought my dream of running was over.

When the coworkers at my new job at St. Anthony's learned of my previous surgery, they coddled me, not allowing me to do anything that might cause a problem with my back. In retrospect I think that reinforced my image of disability, which added to my growing sense of inability and incompleteness. When I came to Portland on my first travel nurse assignment, I chose not to mention my back surgery to these new coworkers. It was eye surgery, and the patients stayed on the same gurney throughout, so lifting wasn't an issue. After being here for a while, a friend invited me to climb Mt. St. Helen's with him; he assured me I could do it. He had completed the climb round-trip in five or six hours. Amy, it was the hardest thing I've ever done next to giving birth and only because it didn't take quite as long. It took me fourteen hours to do the trip. It was about halfway up the mountain that I knew and said to myself, "If I can do this, I can do a marathon." And so I did. And another and another and another. The last as I mentioned was the NYC marathon on my 54th birthday. A friend embroidered "It's my birthday" on my running hat; I had hundreds and hundreds of well wishes that day. My face hurt from grinning for 26.2 miles. Although I finished with a PR (personal record), my time wasn't as good as it could have been because I took the opportunity to "high-five" every kid on the side of the road who stood leaning across the barricade trying to touch as many runners as they could. There was no way I was going to pass up gathering all of that energy. I stopped to share some Tiger Balm ointment with a man who had a leg cramp, I stopped for free hugs when offered, I had one of the top five experiences of my life that day, preceded only by the birth my daughters and their subsequent marriages this year and the Mt. St. Helen's climb that inspired it. It might be eclipsed in October of this year when I run the marathon in Athens, Greece. It's the 2500-year anniversary of the original run that inspired the world. What a celebration that will be.

That's a pretty long-winded, self-indulgent story meant only to act as inspiration for you to see this change in your life as having the

potential for literally anything. And don't forget
Gabe sees everything. Show him well.

Kayna made mention of an important detail: *Maybe through
no fault of my own.* It doesn't matter how we got to this spot,
especially if it's a particularly challenging one. Whether through
our own actions or not, we must first start by *forgiving*: ourselves, others we align with our situation, or the world in general. Practically speaking, to move forward we must stop *staying* where we are: rethinking past mistakes, reliving where we
were and wishing to return, or mourning what we see as lost
opportunity.

Go get 'em: You're the sole architect of your future. Whatever
road you chose, make sure you apply:

1) Plan it out, and *see it* coming to fruition.
2) Not just thought, but *action*.
3) Endure peaks and valleys; be *patient* and keep working.

"The only ones that never lose…are the ones that never play."
— BUD WILKINSON

5

MAKING YOUR MARK

How many successful entrepreneurs reach their goal first time? Who arrives at their passion or purpose without exploring and stumbling?

> Success is not final. Failure is as well not fatal.
> — WINSTON CHURCHILL

You can implement this mentality not only in the arena of sport, but in your daily life as well, by the way you conduct yourself.

1) feel deeply
2) speak honestly
3) help someone
4) impact someone

And one more thing: *"Never give up...never, ever give up!"* That's what Jim Valvano, former coach of the North Carolina State Wolfpack basketball team, said in a speech only weeks before he succumbed to cancer. His fight was noteworthy, and what he gave back in the process was the creation of the "Jimmy V" Foundation to fight all forms of cancer. More than 200 million dollars has been raised from this endeavor. Valvano said in that speech that cancer could ravage his body, but it could never take away his passion, his fight, or what was in his heart.

Indeed, nothing can do this to us, if we refuse to let it.

Go get 'em: You have control over your "never give up" gene. You're the only one who can stop trying!

"If you think you can, you can. And if you think you can't, you're right."

6

OPTIMISM

I'm so fortunate. I have a wonderful mother, whose intelligence and warmth is only rivaled by her effervescent nature. People often comment about her—what a pleasure she is to be around, how infectious her smile is, her great good-naturedness. With all these glistening traits, I comment to most, "The greatest lesson in life she has taught me is to *always be optimistic.*"

Like anyone, my mother has met adversity. She knows what it is like to meet repeated disappointment and tragedy in her lifetime. From the late '60s to early '70s, she lost six siblings and close family members. Even at my young age at the time, I held my breath when the phone rang, especially later into the evenings. It terrified her to get a late-night call; but lifted up by my very supportive father, she stood up and stood strong, making herself aware of the needs of others and then following up by meeting those needs to the best of her ability. She did everything from running the family business when necessary to traveling by bus to Temple, Texas, many consecutive weekends to see my ailing grandmother.

Again, she had support and would be the first one to tell you so. My aunt Liz, her oldest sister, lived in Tyler, Texas. When my grandparents became unable to live on their own, Liz moved them to Tyler to live with her. Liz had already endured enough of her own adversity for a lifetime. Tragedy virtually began at the outset of her marriage in 1957 when my Uncle Lou, her husband and a war veteran, was stricken by Parkinson's disease. He was such a gentle man, a real class act, but it wasn't easy for them. Uncle Lou lived for fifteen years beyond that.

There is no doubt Liz was a real trooper, but the effervescence my mother lent to everything she did was apparent the moment you were in her presence. She'll tell you she was doing "what needed to be done." Her glistening demeanor put her own personal touch on everything, even when immense courage was needed in taking care of a sick relative, surviving the untimely death of a loved one, or dealing with the day-to-day events of partnering with my father in their family business and raising a family.

At the first printing of this book, Ruth Bravo is a vivacious eighty-three-year-old, still imparting that famous "Ruth Bravo verve" she's so well known for and has possessed her entire life. I'm so lucky to have her in my life, and the optimism she exudes is one of the great blessings bestowed upon me. It is undeniable that her attitude toward adversity has led the way to my underlying approach to things—the glass is always three-quarters full. Her view of the world, no matter what difficulties lay in her path, continues to impact me, and for that I'm forever grateful.

Go get 'em: We can't micromanage whom we spend all our time around, but we can decide to "choose" positive people to surround ourselves with.

"The weak can never forgive. Forgiveness
is the attribute of the strong."
— MAHATMA GANDHI

7

PEACE

Optimism is further displayed by allowing yourself to forgive both others and yourself. In most religious traditions, apology, forgiveness, and making amends are highly valued, as evidenced by the formal rituals that for millennia have marked those acts. In Judaism, for example, one of the holiest days of the year is Yom Kippur, the Day of Atonement. Observant Jews fast that day to repent for their transgressions of the past year. Catholics confess their sins to a priest to receive spiritual guidance and forgiveness.

Yoga teaching, too, speaks to the importance of dealing ethically with others. The concept of karma tells us, in part, that our actions will come back to us. Karma yoga is the practice of selflessly putting ourselves in service to others, and part of this is trying to right the wrongs we have done.

Not only does the "do unto others" prophecy come to fruition in terms of happiness, fulfillment, and karmic manifestation: there are also the *health benefits* of forgiveness. When people can't forgive, their stress levels increase, which can contribute to cardiovascular problems. People who are able to practice forgiveness have stronger hearts, lower blood pressure, and better immune responses than those who carry a grudge.

There are measurable health benefits to having an open heart and a clear mind. A sincere apology is a central mechanism to self-forgiveness, however accepted or rebuffed. There are similar health benefits in forgiving ourselves as much as in forgiving other people.

The action, or lack of such, you receive from your apology to others is likely to evoke an emotional response. Feelings of deep relief, re-acquaintance, and gratefulness are, of course, most desired. Inevitably, as we can't control how our apologies are received, this isn't always the case. In the sacred Hindu text Bhagavad Gita, the yogi Arjuna is told that it is a mistake to focus on the results of our efforts instead of on the efforts themselves: "The man who is devoted and not attached to the fruit of his actions obtains tranquility." Most crucial is not that your apology is successful but that you make the effort. The purity of this intention is all you can—*or have the right to*—control.

Go get 'em: There's absolutely "no future" in not always taking the optimists' views. Challenges don't leave, but everything's easier.

"Three things we can control in our lives…our effort, our integrity, and our compassion for others."
— MARK BRAVO

8

INTANGIBLES

This doesn't mean day-to-day and more enduring, problems and issues cease to exist, but *attitude is everything.* You make a profound difference in many lives by how you project yourself. Remember, you've built a reputation of respect that should not only be implemented in the business world. This means that your words, gestures, kindness—the intangibles that define who you are—are like an elixir to the soul of one in need of a lift, encouragement, or even a bit of inspiration.

There is nothing more contagious than a positive attitude. Ever notice how your spirits drop and the air around you becomes "heavier" when all you hear is negative comments? Even if they're not directed at you, tension fills the atmosphere, and one or two dim comments seem to lead to nothing but more of the same. We don't have to live in a fairy tale world to be overridingly positive; we simply practice the positive habit of thinking that way (back to "Practice Good Habits"), and the more we do it, this lifestyle (see "Building Momentum") becomes our "way of life." We continue down the path closer to how we want to live.

This transfers to all areas of our lives (see "Find Success"). Attitude, good or bad, is contagious. So are frame of mind, energy, and adrenalin. These are the building blocks to success. The bonus here is that these intangibles are all up to us; we have the power to move forward, stay stagnant, or go backward (sometimes, stagnancy translates to moving backward).

We can't always affect others' attitudes or mind-sets, but as far as we're concerned, it's squarely up to us! We have a choice each day as to the attitude we adopt for that day. What has transpired, what will happen in the future—it should not be material in forming our attitudes that particular day. We can't change the past, only learn from it, savor it, and move on. What comes to be is out of our control and can't be changed. Our "home court advantage" that cannot be neutralized, downplayed, or hindered by others is our attitude. Things will happen that are out of our control or seem unfair. Even "bad breaks" will inevitably occur. We're in the driver's seat though—not always as to what happens, but how we react to it. Attitude is easily 90 percent of the battle; most things aren't terminal.

Positive attitude is not something to be purchased, or simply wished for. Like an art, it must be practiced, and discipline and stick-to-itiveness shown. A great American middle-distance runner, Lynn Jennings, said, "Mental will is a muscle that needs exercise, just like muscles of the body." It involves a combination of determination and acceptance, which may sound contradictory. Not really.

Those things we can't control that we don't like require acceptance. I approach these instances by calling upon gratitude for things in my life I'm thankful for, some I maybe hadn't even counted on. That "levels the count" and helps extinguish any "woe is me" feeling.

We've all seen prominent people of notable position, wealth, and acclaim who simply don't seem very happy. Either you see this discontent etched on their faces, or it comes through loud and clearly in their actions. The impact of attitude on life cannot be overemphasized. It rises above the past, current circumstances, money, education, and status. In fact, it's no small factor in most any success story.

Attitude is multidimensional. As well as finding the positives when they're well hidden, it involves a determination, sometimes a never-say-die attitude. Thomas Edison was not only the father of inventions but also authored as many quips as he did creations.

> Our greatest weakness lies in giving up. The most certain way to succeed is to try just one more time.

Skill and giftedness are assets surely, but they can be taught. It's what you bring to the table attitude-wise that sets you and your results apart.

———————

Go get 'em: Find your intangibles and nurture them. We all have 'em; they're your edge!

"There seems to be a door on the way to remarkable success that can be passed through only by those willing to persevere beyond the point where the majority stops and turns back."
— EARL NIGHTINGALE

9

GRATITUDE

Gratitude tops the list of all virtues. Without it, there is no happiness in your life. We can *never* be satisfied, *never* be good enough, *never* be fulfilled. It's really that simple.

Adapted from a Melody Beattie comment:

> Gratitude unlocks all you can be. It washes away insecurity, lessens ego, and gives us "permission" to tap the fullness of life. It turns what we have into enough, and more. It turns denial into acceptance, chaos to order, confusion to clarity. With gratitude, we stop to breathe.
>
> It makes us grateful for mere sustenance, then turns that sustenance into a feast. A house becomes a home, and a stranger transforms into a friend. Gratitude brings acceptance to our past, grants us peace for today, and creates a vision for tomorrow.

Go get 'em: Being happy with what you have doesn't mean not striving for more. Do both with grace and passion.

"The greatest thing you'll ever learn is
to love and be loved in return."
— NATALIE COLE

10

ALL ENCOMPASSING

My parents' marriage through my eyes:

When I want to call upon something heartwarming, solid, to be counted on, I always think of my parents—the nearly fifty-five years they spent together. In fact, their relationship not only stood the test of time, it continues to! The respect for my father with which my mother continues to live her life tells me one thing: when a bond is created that's stronger than either of the individuals separately, nothing can impair it—not even one's passing.

I never saw them tired of each other. That seems hard to imagine, as it's very natural to want time away from each other, especially because they worked side-by-side for nearly fifty years. I was fortunate enough to grow up in our business; and being there full-time for almost twenty-five of those years, I saw this play out day to day. I marveled often at how they worked things out, always *as a team*, whether a personal or business decision. My mother has always been a driving force in our family, and in the business, she was an equal partner as well. Interestingly—and a great lesson I learned from them—neither ever had a need, nor even the slightest desire, to take credit for running the show. I must say they were both great bosses!

As my father began to slow down and we were ready for a transition, we sold the business, and taking care of my father became my mother's main focus. She taught me another great lesson: compassion. There was never a time during this roughly five-year period when she showed any impatience or she gave less effort. Not that I expected *anything* different, but seeing a different aspect of their love grow in my father's last years touched me in a way I'll never forget. Since Dad's passing in 2003, this unrelenting love shines every bit as strong in my mother. She misses him every single day, but the dignity with which she sets an example never wanes. It's one of the greatest sources of pride I call upon as I move through life.

My parents were very fortunate; they found each other, and it was as perfect a life as one could ever imagine. Also though, they were a team, and everything about their lives, their actions toward each other and others, their examples set, stated that loud and clearly. When you believe in something deeply, let it be an all-encompassing commitment and be willing to ride through any "peaks and valleys" that arise. They not only are inevitable, but they strengthen and "raise your game."

Just as with an individual, it's true with a couple: there's no greater example to be set than the impact you have while on this earth. There were many wonderful couples whose examples I grew up learning at least a bit from. Each illustrates that you can leave your mark on your children and those you touch in lasting ways you may not even realize. Whether teaching how to live and treat others by what you do, not what you say, or by honoring your mate every day of your life, you transcend simply the people you directly touch. With these couples, it's a legacy that continues to teach us what is really important.

The fifth commandment states: *honor your father and your mother.*

My parents, to put it succinctly, make me proud to be a *Bravo.*

Go get 'em: Live by example! Someone's always watching and learning.

"When we choose not to focus on what is missing from our lives but are grateful for the abundance that's present...this is life to its fullest."

11   🏃

GRATITUDE FIRST...AND ALWAYS

That's it! We all face adversity in our life. However, it's not the adversity but how we react to it that will determine the joy and happiness in our lives. During tough times, do we spend too much time feeling sorry for ourselves, or can we, with gratitude, learn how to dance in the rain? It almost sounds too simple to feel important, but one word, *gratitude*, can change your attitude, thus, your life, forever.

Thinking we can "control" all the forces that affect us, thus insulating ourselves from surprises, trials...the tests that face everyone, is a losing game! These adversities are actually opportunities for growth. They build our patience, determination, and those *intangibles* such as stick-to-itiveness and *gratitude*.

I think there's no more important trait than *gratitude*. No matter *what else* we possess in terms of talent, intelligence, and sheer drive, we don't *get it* if we don't open our hearts continually to what we do possess. This doesn't speak of physical, hard assets, but the love, relationships, and overall good fortune that inherently exist in our lives. This is gratitude, and it doesn't translate to an occasional "thank you" or dozen roses. It's what we feel inside and, thus, exude to those around us.

We may require internal "reminders" to tap this "attitude of gratitude" from time to time. That's okay. The great result of this way of thinking is that, like with everything we practice, the more repetition—in this case, remembering the many opportunities and blessings we possess—the more "way of life" the event becomes. In other words, this gratitude becomes imbedded in our psyche, and we live in that world immensely more often.

While we adopt this new mind-set not for personal gain, in

terms of gaining assets, being liked more, or even being recognized for this view of life, it just happens! There exists an "aura" around people who genuinely are filled with gratefulness. They inherently give back to the world; they're more altruistic-thinking…they in fact "shine." And in the process, this benefits not only everyone around them, or those aware enough to take notice, but their lives are immensely better by definition. How can they be happier people?

When you accept what comes your way that is out of your control, even when it's not to your liking, you're more equipped to deal with it, to "put your own signature on the project." You raise the calibration of the world around you by lifting virtually everyone you touch in some way. A positive attitude, an encouraging word that you deliver to someone, even a stranger, has a result you may never have imagined. You may not even *know* you're having that impact. This is not important; that you did so is.

When one *allows* enlightenment, remember, it's already inside us; we simply must relax and shed the "principles of hindrance." The entire aura around that person is filled with grace, and people know it. This transforms you to one who draws people toward you, even with no conscious effort on your part.

Go get 'em: Create an aura around you, consciously or by living a principled life. People will notice and flock to you.

"Do what you can, with what you have, where you are...*right now*."
— THEODORE ROOSEVELT

12 🏃

BALANCE

We get caught up in our own lives and subconsciously feel we're the only ones going through something. This is precisely the point where our altruistic nature should take over. It's a "win-win" situation. We get outside ourselves and are empowered to confront whatever arises.

Our time is our most valuable asset.

What we do with this most precious of assets dictates our level of accomplishment, gratification, and ultimate peace of mind. There is nothing we can attain or strive for that remotely should be valued, with the exception of our close relationships, as we do our time and what we do with it. You can rationalize that you made money, accomplished all of your appointments, and "clocked in" every day, but living to the fullest is what sets you apart. This means appreciating things properly, honoring others, and respecting yourself and others. These traits should be inherent. Sometimes due to one's past or the lack of guidance, they're not. Remember though, they can still be learned and practiced every day.

Do your homework, follow-through, and leave no stone unturned. Balance is a key ingredient. You can give everything to a project, goal, *moment*...and still enjoy, respect, and honor others, and your commitments to them.

Go get 'em: Communicate as clearly as you can! When you're respectful and credible, people will appreciate your straight-forwardness.

"The quality of one's life lies in direct proportion to their commitment."
—VINCE LOMBARDI

13

TEAM

REALIZE THE POWER OF "WE"':
Mental, Physical, and Emotional "Vitamins"

Teamwork is essential to nurturing, sometimes even creating, much of the successes we achieve. A good leader will recognize this and be willing to empower those under her to grow and feel their own successes through three key initiatives:

1) Giving responsibility for key decisions freely when that trust is earned.
2) Acknowledging and rewarding positive moves by those under your watch.
3) Recognizing the goal as more important than individual credit and furthering this philosophy to the *team*.

Go get 'em: Everyone is rewarded when it's a joint effort. Whether at home or work, place priority on the *team*.

"Failure is not fatal, but failure to change might be."
— JOHN WOODEN

14

THE NECESSITY OF CHANGE

The road to fulfillment is rarely offered as a straight line. As a leader, deciding to make changes is the easy part. Getting your people on board is much more difficult. The first reaction is usually a resounding, *"Oh no! What comes now?"*

Why is that? Quite simply, change is an emotional process. We are all creatures of habit; I know I am. Most seek routine. At the very least, for most of us, our "comfort zone" is craved, and unchartered waters are scary! That's not always counter-productive, but *inevitably* our boat is rocked, either from within or externally. While not always able to greet this newness with a welcome mat, we should be open to what can be gained and *learned* from it. As importantly, we find out what's inside us. How we accept what's thrown our way in life tells us what we're made up of: *we don't just build character through adversity; we find out what kind of character we possess.*

> Some change when they see the light,
> others only when they feel the heat.

The truth, of course, is that change can be a wonderful gift. In fact, it is the key that unlocks the doors to growth and excitement in any organization. Most important, without it, your competition will pass you by. A big part of success, as a leader, will be your ability to inspire your team to get out of their comfort zones, to assure them that even though they are on a new path, it's the right path, for the right reasons.

Go get 'em: Go ahead; dread it, deny it, ignore it...*change* happens anyway. Make it work *for* you; be open to the best way to embrace it, and think of the possibilities!

"We make a living by what we get…we make a *life* by what we give."
— WINSTON CHURCHILL

15

IMPACT

I was painfully shy as a child. That may seem hard to believe since I am a mentor and speaker today. However, first grade was daunting to me, and my concerns were not quickly relieved. At the beginning of the day, all of the children walked in and sat down in "the circle." I wasn't that forthcoming. I would sit on the piano bench each day, somewhat removed from the circle. I have wondered why the teacher showed me so much patience and handled my shyness differently than she treated the other children, who were more indoctrinated to this transition than I. I don't know why, but she did. This same behavior carried on late into the year. I was not a participant in life. I was an observer. I didn't know how to get in the game, and worse, I didn't want in the game. Then one day everything changed.

One of these most pivotal of moments in my life occurred when a man named Ben Shanker stepped out of his busy schedule and "played catch" with me. As a young boy, I wasn't aware that Ben was such a successful person. I wasn't aware of his vast accomplishments. I was only aware that Ben was willing to play catch, and I loved playing football. Ben was an incredibly busy man, and I'm sure he had many things he could have been doing that day.

To Ben, it was one small, unmonumental moment, but it was *the* moment that changed the course of my life. I don't know if my personality changed by leaps and bounds that day, but Ben did something that I can only describe as giving my life an early-stage *definition*. Ben created positive momentum for me, where it was needed, and showed me I could do the same for others. Anyone can! By taking a moment out of *his* day, a corridor opened to a myriad of things possible in life.

I'm sure Ben didn't know the simple act of playing catch with me would have such a dramatic effect, and I know he wasn't aware what would eventuate, but a few things in my life had changed with that moment.

Ben taught me compassion, and with it, the momentum in my life had begun. I moved from the piano bench to the inner circle, and I never looked back. On rare occasions I have mentioned this to Ben, and the modesty that he has always displayed shines through each time. I hope Ben Shanker now knows the true impact he had upon me on a day nearly 50 years ago, and that he still has.

Go get 'em: Dance like no one's watching, but *live your life* as if everybody is!

"The best and most beautiful things in the world cannot be seen or even touched. They must be felt within the heart."
— HELEN KELLER

16

REPAIRING THE WORLD

Now my passion is to impact the lives of others through fitness and through their mind-sets. Either with a specific aspiration, a defined course, or by daily actions, we all have the capacity to have impact. In that way, whether noticed by the masses or only our small circles, we can bring repair to the world. In Judaism, this phrase is used often "*tikkun olam*" (to repair the world).

In short, these words speak to two true roles humanity can play in the quality of all existence: to help those in need and to "do the right thing" in all phases of life. Living a life of *examples*, not of *explanation*.

My father never understood my love of sports, but he always understood that to take care of his family he had to take care of himself. With the pawnshop needing constant attention, he had the perfect excuse to stop working out. He purposely chose to go to the YMCA and work out for about an hour and half, come rain or shine. He lived out the importance of that in front of me.

Whether you're an elite athlete or an athlete at heart, don't allow things that are important to you, and important to your life's momentum, to be at the mercy of the "urgencies" placed in your path. Ask yourself if that particular sidebar is drawing you closer to your goal or further from your goal. If it is not drawing you closer to your goal, then at that time it must be discarded.

Stay vigilant and watch for those people who either consciously or subconsciously want you to fail to make themselves feel better about where they are in their own lives. Their envy of your success can manifest itself in a form of discouragement that may work to stop your momentum. Sadly, this is often disguised as excuses for their own behaviors or negative comments or concerns about yours. You might recognize it in comments such as "I would lift weights, but I just don't want to get too big," or "I would run, but I heard it is just too hard on your body and you'll regret it later in life." Learn to recognize these conversational red flags as sidebars, as clutter, that are stumbling blocks to your positive momentum.

My father had a passion to take care of his family and to take care of his body. He didn't allow pressure, emotions, or other people to make his decisions for him. He made sure the things that mattered most came before the things that mattered least.

My dad didn't share my passion for going to Owen Field to watch OU football games. He felt he had the "best seat in the house" in his own home, his easy chair, with his drink right beside him and the television right in front of him. I couldn't imagine at the time missing a game. Now I am the same age as my father was then, and guess what? I enjoy the game from my easy chair, sitting right in front of my television.

Don't think you have to be a public figure, or even make known your actions of compassion or humanity, to make your mark in this world.

I've seen many times where one person has made a profound impact on another, or group of people, with a quiet act of respect, kindness, or altruism. These are the deeds that help us "repair the world" in our own way.

If Dad were here, he would smile at the way the moments in his life have become my lifestyle. Thanks, Dad.

Go get 'em: Find your "righteous mind," the way you lend impact to the world. Never doubt you can have tremendous impact through small gestures, and from the time you do, the ripple effect begins! You may not even know it did, but that's not important.

"All things entail rising and falling timing.
You must be able to discern this."
— MIYAMOTO MUSASHI

17

TIMING

My father and mother were married fifty-four years when my father passed away. I didn't get married until I was fifty-two years old. My parents had a great marriage, and marriage was a serious commitment on my behalf. I knew from watching my parents what that vow meant, and when I married, I knew it would be forever, but timing is everything.

There was a beautiful girl at Northeast High School in Oklahoma City, Oklahoma. I admired her from afar. Yet if there was a metaphorical piano bench, I was sitting on it. We had a mutual agreement between us. I was afraid to talk to her, and she didn't know I was alive. It is hard for a romance to flourish under those harsh conditions.

As time passed, I became more and more involved in the goals I set for myself, and running came to the forefront in my life. I had only myself to care for, and I could give all of my attention and time to the path I laid before me.

People often want to know how I got started running, and I must tell you that it was somewhat inherent. It seems that from early on, I *ran* everywhere I went—to school, on errands for my parents from our store, when I got out of the car at the grocery… It's just what I did.

The fact that basketball was my passion as a youngster, my very favorite pastime, didn't hurt my pursuit of running. As I was always the shortest on the court, speed was integral to survival. Beyond college, a buddy asked me to join him in a six-mile race. I said I would, but having as a steady running regimen two to three miles (as hard as I could) didn't fill me with confidence. I figured I'd run the first half of the race in about eighteen minutes and the last half in roughly the rest of the afternoon. Well, craziest thing. I was patient, and the race went better than I ever dreamed.

From that experience was born my love of the sport as a "lifetime" discipline. There came a time when I realized that if I wanted to progress, I couldn't stop the forward motion. Then it hit me; I realized I was at a crossroads.

I decided the marathon would be next. Well, not next, but "down the road" (metaphorically speaking). I needed a plan, and even as a novice, knew this goal couldn't be reached "tomorrow." The first big barrier I had to cross, physically *and* mentally, was the ten-mile mark. I hadn't crossed that bridge before, and it would be a clear confidence-builder if I did so, in an intact fashion (translated: *knowing my name* when I finished). The other thing: I only knew one speed—not all-out, but hard and consistent. I wanted to run ten miles as fast as I was already running. This created some trepidation, if not fear, as the day I had planned neared. The moment I decided to run ten miles was as big a breakthrough as running that first mile or the marathon.

I had a stomachache the rest of the day from the effort, and that day continues to rank as a "top ten moment" in my life.

I finally realized that if I wanted to be a marathoner, I needed to stop worrying about time frames and keep my focus advancing toward that achievement. Progress was progress, and this was something I had clear control over. My career as a marathoner began, and I envisioned for the first time really doing it. I would simply have to choose my moment.

I was born to be a runner, to be in continuous forward movement, and to keep my goals fluid. While those are all good traits, the characteristic of perpetual motion didn't serve me well when my life crossed paths once again with that beautiful girl from Northeast High School. Older and wiser didn't make up for my uncertainty and lack of commitment. To be honest, I was comfortable living my life my way.

Although Leslie and I dated for quite some time, as fate would have it, I wasn't through with the journey I had to take. I moved to California for a while, and that detour might be seen as momentum lost, but things aren't always as they appear. You can't always take the straight road; you must choose the path that is right for you. Yet in life, just as in a marathon, it is accomplished one step at a time.

There is a path you must take to cross the finish line, and there is no promise that the path will be easy. In fact, why would you think it would be easy? There is seldom a time when everything feels perfect. It is always going to be a little too cold or a little too windy, or the hill will seem too steep. As with any great accomplishment in life, we must guard against attitudes of entitlement. We must realize that it will take work and it will take diligence to cross that line. It won't happen by accident.

Sometimes that path leads to heartache. There are losses along the way. When I moved to California, at Leslie's encouragement I might add, a loss occurred, and it was one of those moments. Leslie had a broken heart, but she is an honest person, and she respects herself enough to make sure we were on the right path, not just the easy path.

When you want to accomplish something in life, there are people who will always encourage you to take the easy route. They will want you to skip your training; they will want you to get caught up in the clutter—things that work to reverse your momentum.

Leslie isn't one of those people. She wanted us to take the right path, and I did too. It wasn't easy, but when my path led me back to Oklahoma, I made a decision. I chose to decide what was really important in my life and how I wanted to live out my future.

Leslie's heart was eventually able to heal, and I began to realize what I had felt, but not acted upon, for years. We were meant to be together. We might not have as many years as my mother and father had, but we can have the quality of marriage they had.

Timing *is* everything, and in spite of the unconventional road taken to get here, no, *because* of it, I have no doubt that our journey brought us to this time of great joy *at just the right time*.

When Leslie and I had that fateful conversation, the timing was right, and our path was set. I have made a firm commitment to take care of Leslie all the days of our lives, and I won't falter, for she is truly the prize of my life.

Go get 'em: When one of those "lifetime" decisions come your way, treat it differently than your other choices. Bring your key senses into play: your mind and your *heart*.

"Today is the tomorrow you worried about yesterday."
— DALE CARNEGIE

18

NOW

One of my greatest flaws? Being present. I know that may seem *disconnected* when you read it, but it is true. You have to be aware of life around you. You must be present. What may seem insignificant and small to you may change someone else's life. Don't downplay that and don't forget that.

In yoga practice, being present is being *mindful*. This relates to taking in all that your body is feeling. It is being cognizant that you are breathing with ease and relaxing consciously the muscle or part of the body engaged as you reach the apex of the stretch, position, or pose. These "resets" of easy breathing and this aspiring to normal length and tension of muscles and tendons brought into play in yoga is a great analogy of how we might practice our approach to life. Very little adversity is terminal, and if we breathe in the beauty, joy, and *opportunity*, we consistently experience, we'll outlast any short-term setbacks that might otherwise derail us from our chosen paths.

For example, since my hip replacement, I still run and will continue to run, but I can't necessarily run for long periods at the rate and speed that I was used to. While this took some mental adjustment on my part, I came to terms with several factors related to this. I had to understand that momentum was about reaching the finish line with my personal best...effort that is, and not comparing that to someone else's or any performance from the past.

I am often approached after a race, the other runner visiting with me about his or her race. I find myself in a continuous state of surprise when that happens as I am not the fastest runner in the race. I wonder why they come to ask me questions when it is quite obvious that while I do well, I am not the leader of the pack.

I visited with my wife, Leslie, about this, and she said it was because I am approachable. People realize that I care. If someone is being so kind as to ask my opinion or share his or her thoughts with me, I honestly *do* care!

When these moments occur, I want to make sure I stop and engage in the conversation. I don't want to take the moment walking. Slowing down my momentum for that brief few minutes is actually moving forward for me and for the other person!

Go get 'em: Only you hold the template for happiness in your life: not others, not possessions, not fame or acclaim. Take ownership of your life. Value what you give to the world. Make it positive and make it count!

"The pursuit of *excellence* is not a goal; it's a habit."
— BOOKER T. WASHINGTON

19

SELF-DISCIPLINE

Self-discipline is the key to personal greatness. It is the magic quality that opens all doors for you and makes everything else possible. With self-discipline, the average person can rise as far and as fast as his talents and intelligence can take him. Yet without a solid dose of this trait, a person with every blessing of background, education, and opportunity will seldom rise above mediocrity.

I have heard coaches in little league baseball tell pitchers and catchers during a game just to "play catch" so they would calm down. The two positions practice day in and day out during all those warm spring afternoons and evenings, but then something happens. The game steps in and the intensity increases. Emotions run high, and a ball thrown in practice seems to be but a distant memory.

The pitcher steps up to the mound and stares down at the glove of his catcher, squatted with his arm up and extended out to him. He watches for the signals, and then the ball is released with force as the two work together as a team to end the batter's chances before they start. With each ball thrown, the pitcher focuses on results, but the basics learned and practiced come back into play, subconsciously but ever-present. With the bases loaded and the batter up to the plate, the pitcher and the catcher embrace the intensity of the moment and allow all of these practices to take over. First and foremost, remembering the love of the game.

BARGAINING AS A TACTIC
Yes, I definitely think "bargaining" should be included, and I

have indeed talked about it often. How we use this tactic, mainly to "fake it 'til you make it" that builds momentum and gets us to our original goal? Also, when in conjunction, implemented with the "kinder, gentler" approach, bargaining allows us the grace to realize that "part of the way gets us closer than not moving at all" and lays the *groundwork* for the necessary fortitude next time around.

Go get 'em: In determining that your life has the meaning you'd hoped for, compliments are nice. Look, however, inside your heart for the answer. If not, it's not too late!

"Things that are given to us for nothing we place little value on. Things that we pay money for, we value. The paradox is that exactly the reverse is true. Everything that's really worthwhile in life came to us free. Our minds, our souls, our bodies, our hopes, our dreams, our ambitions, our intelligence, our love of family and children and friends and country—all these priceless possessions are free. But the things that cost us money are actually very cheap and can be replaced at any time. A good man can be completely wiped out and make another fortune. He can do that several times. Even if a home burns down, we can rebuild it. But the things we got for nothing can never be replaced."
— EARL NIGHTINGALE

20

SEASONS

A story told to me that is one of those lessons life seems to hand you now and then, if you'll watch and listen.

"You see, I sat down one day and did a little arithmetic. The average person lives about seventy-five years. I know, some live more and some live less; but on average, folks live about seventy-five years.

"Now then, I multiplied seventy-five times fifty-two, and I came up with thirty-nine hundred, which is the number of Saturdays that the average person has in their entire lifetime. Now, stick with me, I'm getting to the important part.

"It took me until I was fifty-five years old to think about all this in any detail," he went on, "and by that time, I had lived through over twenty-eight hundred Saturdays. I got to thinking that if I lived to be seventy-five, I only had about a thousand of them left to enjoy. So I went to a toy store and bought every single marble they had. I ended up having to visit three toy stores to round up one thousand marbles. I took them home and put them inside a large, clear plastic container right here in the shack next to my gear.

"Every Saturday since then, I have taken one marble out and thrown it away. I found that by watching the marbles diminish, I focused more on the really important things in life.

"There's nothing like watching your time here on this earth run out to help get your priorities straight.

"I hope you spend more time with your family, and I hope to meet you again, Mark.

"Now let me tell you one last thing before I sign off with you and take my lovely wife out for breakfast. This morning, I took the very last marble out of the container. I figure that if I make it until next Saturday, then I have been given a little extra time. And the one thing we can all use is a little more time."

How often do you think someone has, as his time on earth was nearing an end, thought to himself, *I wish I'd have spent a little more time in the office?*

The best way to explain a life "well lived" is by no words at all. It's spending your days in such a manner as to be missed when you're gone. When your memory is relived time and time again, your legacy is enduring; and when you're spoken of fondly—even moving people to emotion when thinking of you—I believe one of the greatest things occur: You remain with the people you've touched in a transcendent manner that never goes away.

Let me tell you a story about a woman who came into my family's life just before I was born. My three sisters—Jan, Joan, and Vikki—had arrived already, and as near newborns, my parents needed help with them, as my mother joined my dad working in the store.

Melissa came to us as a housekeeper but quickly became much more. In a matter of months she was considered "family" and had full "rights of refusal" when my parents hired a nanny to spend the night with us. If they weren't in our best interest, she fired them without hesitation.

Melissa had no formal education yet was the best "stand-up comic" I've ever seen. She also had a sense of what was right for us and in the world in general, and she never wavered in her beliefs, though her life was filled with frequent hardship.

As a black woman born prior to 1920 and growing up in Oklahoma City, Melissa had a lot to contend with. Her grace in dealing with the cards dealt, her willingness to "join" our family (integral in our lives for over fifty years), and the humor and life lessons she taught us all left an indelible mark in our hearts, and she continues to be a topic of conversation when we gather, though she's been gone five years at the time of the first printing of this book.

Her compassion was incredible. She knew just what to do to make you feel better, evoke a laugh, or teach a lesson. When Vikki cooked green eggs, Joan and Jan brought dogs home they claimed had "followed" them, or my mother or aunts needed advice on something, Melissa was there.

I felt such comfort from simply being around her that virtually my entire senior year in high school I came home at midday to share a tuna and baked beans lunch and watch soap opera with her. Sure, I liked the shows, but I wonder if she knew why I really came home each day.

Melissa had very little in the way of hard assets when she passed away, but the life she made for herself was overflowing, and her impact eternal. Melissa was grateful for us, and we owe her beyond measure.

Go get 'em: Make your life count. Respect your responsibilities, honor your friends, and cherish your family or whomever fills that spot, as if the clock is running. It is!

"Hope is a good breakfast but a bad supper."
— FRANCIS BACON, SR.

21

STRIVE

When things aren't going right, or you're having a tough time feeling any sense of success within your life, a kick-start early in the day can change your entire perspective and catapult your momentum to last the entire day. This can simply mean fulfilling a day's agenda when it seems unattainable. A single mother, a busy executive, someone taking on two jobs to make ends meet—tremendously adverse lives, yet all face the same pursuit. Sometimes just getting through is enough for that day. Then again, at some point most all of us need to challenge ourselves to move forward, to ask more of ourselves.

How do we do it? How do we bring positive momentum to our day from its outset, and set the tone for a day well lived. Maybe it begins with twenty-five pushups, or just one, or it can be having breakfast every day. Anything that helps us feel closer to *the best we can be* opens the floodgates for just that to happen.

> To succeed...you need to find something to hold on to, something to motivate you, something to inspire you.
> —TONY DORSETT,
> *Heisman Trophy winner*

Get outside yourself; do one thing, say one thing that makes the day better for someone else.

> The race is not always to the swift, but to those who keep on running.
> — NIKE POSTER

Go get 'em: Real competitors love tough competition. They're fair, but they demand from themselves more than anyone else. Maybe competitors exist in a more awakened state and give back more to society. Are you a "competitor"?

"You have to know how to accept
rejection and reject acceptance."
—RAY BRADBURY

22

STORMS

Standing in against the fire—only by going through adversity do we *really* get to see *if* we've grown, *how* we've grown. It's the best way to know we're moving forward. This doesn't mean you should seek out danger simply to see what you're made of. I'm not saying you should stand on the side of a mountain and dangle one leg over the edge. We get enough opportunity for growth day-to-day. It's more about being ready when you're challenged and staying focused and positive when things happen that test our resolve.

These tests come in many forms. When you're faced with twenty things to do *right now* and more inclined to throw up your hands and do nothing, take a positive action.

> If it's free, it's advice; if you pay for it, it's counseling; if you can use either one, it's a miracle.
> — JACK ADAMS

Boil down what is most timely to accomplish, most pivotal, most *terminal*. It can be staying determined and keeping the pedal down when you're completely out of gas running a race. The victory *becomes* the journey! Never underestimate the momentum that swings your way by just one positive action taken.

Go get 'em: Always be prepared to "break through." *Enthusiasm* is the energy and force that builds momentum of the soul and mind.

"By failing to prepare you are preparing to fail."
— BENJAMIN FRANKLIN

23 🏃

TESTS

Pressure: when the task at hand exceeds one's level of preparation

This is where *we* have control over our future, our thoughts, our actions, our results. If we do the work, why fear what's to come? If we've not yet prepared, the "fake it 'til you make it" mind-set can work immeasurably in our favor. There's no excuse for work ethic, but if we've not yet been able to do our diligence, make sure expectations are realistic. Then let confidence, breathing, and relaxation techniques spoken of previously, and maybe *most* importantly stick-to-itiveness, see us through 'til we can "level the playing field" with preparation.

The only *legitimate* pressure we face can be summed up in a quote by the legendary distance runner Steve Prefontaine, one-time holder of every American distance record from two miles to ten kilometers. Over an all-too-short career that ended tragically when he died in a car accident in 1975, at age twenty-four, Prefontaine became arguably the most well-known American runner in the sport's history, not only because of his talent, but how he approached running and his sheer love of the sport. When he stated, "To give anything less than your best is to sacrifice *the gift,*" he spoke to not only the arena of athletics, but to life as a whole.

> It's not the will to win that matters—everyone has
> that. It's the will to prepare to win that matters.
> — PAUL "BEAR" BRYANT

If we know down deep that we've prepared, executed, and shown proper tenacity when the situation called for that, we can take what comes with a clear conscience. We possess peace of mind, and with it, we are energized to take on what next lies ahead.

If instead we're backpedaling, taking short cuts, admitting to ourselves we've not done the work but hoping to slip by, are we *really* able to achieve peace within ourselves and build upon that?

———————————

Go get 'em: Do the little things that "train" you for success, not just the fun stuff. Spectacular achievements are always preceded by unspectacular preparation.

"Opportunity is missed by most because it is
dressed in overalls and looks like work."
— THOMAS EDISON

24

LUCK: WHEN YOU'RE PRIMED, IT FINDS YOU

How easy it is to think that one who has been blessed with more luck, good fortune has an easier path than ourselves? All we must do is look around for someone who seemingly has more "trappings," and if that's the "be all, end all" for you, usually immediate disheartenment follows closely behind.

Time better spent when something pivotal is on the line is to be prepared for whatever the task at hand may hold and make the most of that time spent. Explore every avenue where something might be asked of you. It's homework, diligence, knowing what's applicable and where you need not spend time.

> What matters most should not be left to the mercy
> of what matters least.
> — MARK BRAVO

Know where your efforts should be best extended, and do all you can to ready yourself for the pivotal moment: the meeting, the game, the encounter. This training is your rite of passage, and in most cases writes the script for game day.

Enjoy the journey, for the knowledge you gain can be measured in ways that extend beyond the task at hand, to other venues, for the rest of your life.

Go get 'em: Don't stare so long at a closed door that you see too late the one that is open.

"Change is the essence of life. Be willing to surrender what you are for what you could become."

25

SURRENDER

A truly surrendered person may *look* passive, especially when something appears to need doing, and everyone around is shouting, "Get a move on! Get it done! This is urgent!" Seen in perspective, however, what looks like inaction is often simply a recognition that now is not the time to act.

We gain strength from the *"kinder, gentler"* approach. Masters of surrender tend to be masters of flow, knowing intuitively how to move with the energies at play in a situation—and when. You advance when the doors are open, when a stuck situation can be turned, moving subtly down the stream that lets you avoid obstructions and unnecessary confrontations.

We all experience such crossroads when we seem inexorably stuck, not able to move forward.

My miracle-of-surrender stories are rarely as dramatic as the tales you hear of scientists who move from impasse to breakthrough discovery or of accident victims who put their lives in the hands of the universe and live to tell the tale. Nonetheless, it's clear to me that each time I genuinely surrender—that is, stop struggling for a certain result, release the "holding" in my psychic muscles, let go of my control freak's clutch on reality, and place myself in the hands of who I sometimes call my higher power—doors open in both the inner and outer worlds. Tasks I couldn't do become easier. States of peace and intuition that eluded me show up on their own.

Go get 'em: Life is an amazing thing. One dream could change it completely. Only surrender your hindrances; embrace what is left.

"All compromise is based on give and take, but there can be no give and take on fundamentals. Any compromise on mere fundamentals is a surrender. For it is all give and no take."
—MOHANDAS GANDHI

26

YOU WIN

When we allow the human spirit to speak out and let go of such built-in roadblocks as ego and perception, we start the process of really living, and we automatically are closer to the potential we're met for.

It's the fear that something might not go right that keeps us from being able to give our best shot to the project, our physical efforts, or our families. When we break through that fear, it's a quality implementation of confidence...*ego*, if you will, not misplaced boastfulness.

This is not to say there is no value—and sometimes no choice—in learning how to give way. Letting go can be looked at as weakness, yet really it is the "allowance in" of the purest aspects of life: change, acceptance, and trust. We normally see surrender as acquiescing to someone, either when appropriate or out of necessity. Yet the surrender that shifts the platform of your life, that brings a real breakthrough, is something else altogether. True surrender is never to a person, but always to the higher, deeper will, a "way of life" so to speak. This is the recipe:

1) One part loss of ego
2) Large dose of humility
3) Realization that when you give a little, you win a lot.

The more you investigate surrender as a practice, as a tactic, and as a way of being, the more you realize that it isn't what you thought it to be. *Surrender*—as in an old war movie—is not losing! However, if you're like most, this does not ensure the idea is easy to embrace.

––––––––––––––

Go get 'em: "Freedom is the open window through which pours the sunlight of the human spirit and human dignity." – Herbert Hoover

PART TWO
PART TWO
PART TWO
PART TWO

CHARACTER

"All the art of living lies in a fine mingling
of letting go and holding on."
—HENRY ELLIS

27

FLOW

To let life flow, and accept or surrender where things are out of our hands, seems a bit idyllic at first glance. Sounds like something straight from the Dalai Lama, the Buddhist spiritual leader, doesn't it? Not apropos to today's "immediate gratification" lifestyle most pursue, right? Actually though, this "chasing our tails" approach is *not* something most of us really embrace; we simply have been conditioned to this approach.

Try uncluttering your mind with pros and cons before acting or breathing or accepting or *living*; just be and let be...again, how idyllic, right? Well, once the judgment relinquishes its position as the backdrop for your life, you'll be amazed how freeing it is, and how much easier everything comes. It turns into a *flow*.

Most transformational moments—spiritual, creative, or personal—involve this sequence of intense effort, frustration, and then letting go. The effort, the slamming against walls, the intensity and the exhaustion, the fear of failure balanced against the recognition that it is not okay to fail—all these are part of the process by which a human being breaks out of the cocoon of human limitation and becomes willing on the deepest level to open to the infinite power that we all have in our core. It's the same process whether we're mystics, artists, or people trying to solve a difficult life problem. You've probably heard the story of how Einstein, after years of doing the math, had the special theory of relativity downloaded into his consciousness in a moment of stillness. Then there are those that struggle to find an answer or solution to a problem, only to give up just before finding it.

Then miraculously (or so it seems) they find themselves in that spot where their moves and words are natural and right. By releasing the fear, restraint, and expectations that are subconsciously all too often a part of our makeup, one can explore the potential inside.

Go get 'em: You can get to the other side. Know you'll see the hard times through, and be better for it.

"Don't let the fear of striking out hold you back."
— BABE RUTH

28

FEAR OR FEAR NOT?

The nest of young eagles hung on every word as the Master Eagle described his exploits. This was an important day for the eaglets. They were preparing for their first solo flight from the nest. It was the confidence builder many of them needed to fulfill their destiny.

"How far can I travel?" asked one of the eaglets.

"How far can you see?" responded the Master Eagle.

"How high can I fly?" quizzed the young eaglet.

"How far can you stretch your wings?" asked the old eagle.

"How long can I fly?" the eaglet persisted.

"How far is the horizon?" the mentor rebounded.

"How much should I dream?" asked the eaglet.

"How much can you dream?" smiled the older, wiser eagle.

"How much can I achieve?" the young eagle continued.

"How much can you believe?" the old eagle challenged.

Frustrated by the banter, the young eagle demanded, "Why don't you answer my questions?"

"I did."

"Yes. But you answered them with questions."

"I answered them the best I could."

"But you're the Master Eagle. You're supposed to know everything. If you can't answer these questions, who can?"

"You," the old wise eagle reassured.

"Me? How?" The young eagle was confused.

"No one can tell you how high to fly or how much to dream. It's different for each eagle. Only God and you know how far you'll go. You alone will answer that. The only thing that limits you is the edge of your imagination."

The young eagle, puzzled by this, asked, "What should I do?"

"Look to the horizon, spread your wings, and fly."

––––––––––––––

Go get 'em: No one on this earth knows your potential, or what's truly in your heart, but you. Prove the naysayers wrong.

"Go confidently in the direction of your dreams.
Live the life you have imagined."
—THOREAU

29

SELFLESSNESS

Accept *small gains* from where measurable results are born. *Gratitude* can be the start; it can erase selfishness and rid you of lethargy. You're inspired physically, and your spirits are raised.

When we perceive things as not going well, this is manifested in feelings of self-absorption, even self-pity, and this leads to a "woe is me" outlook that can become all consuming. We must detour it immediately. This is accomplished by thinking not of what we don't have or haven't accomplished, but instead of what we *have*, what we *are* capable of, and how lucky we are. We all truly *are* fortunate, for only looking outside our door shows us the multitudes that have much less in their lives than we do. And this not only speaks to material items, but the capabilities, however different, we all possess.

One way to achieve this is to *get outside yourself.* By giving a little of yourself, you lighten your own burdens. Lending a helping hand can show you that you perhaps don't have it as bad as you think you do. Giving of yourself to others can inspire new ways to lead your own life.

Go get 'em: It's always darkest before the dawn. Do something good for someone else, and go to sleep. When you awaken, things will look different.

"In order to engage in battle without compromise, you must find a place within yourself where success and failure do not matter..."

30

WHERE TO?

The first step is to turn the tide, swing *momentum* back your way. How? First, just *breathe*. Then look toward one of your strengths, and use it. It might be your ability to make others feel good, simply by communicating with them. Maybe doing some pushups invigorates you, gets adrenaline going, and kick-starts the process. It can be that "innocent" an act.

> What you get done they can't take away from you.

Getting down the road when you feel stalled can come very deliberately. Nonetheless, this is most meaningful and the springboard for future breakthroughs. Always to *aim higher* is essential. Taking the next step that inspires you breathes life into your day. Back to the point of this chapter, *getting outside yourself* reminds you of all your talents to be called upon. You find yourself rid of the lethargy that only recently seemed so paralyzing.

Don't let ego derail your ability to learn from others. What you are about to say, you already know. So why don't you listen instead?

Go get 'em: "If I am walking with two other men, each of them will serve as my teacher. I will pick out the good points of the one and imitate them, and the bad points of the other and correct them in myself." — Confucius

"Life's too short to live the same day twice…"

31

BEGINNINGS

Keep these thoughts in mind:

We will be known forever by the tracks we leave.

This Native American proverb speaks volumes, both practically and spiritually. If we always have imbedded in our minds that our actions and treatment of others are our legacy, we create an inner "barometer" of how to conduct ourselves.

If as well we see our time here as a springboard for those to come, a positive one if we respect others and the land we occupy, then we treat everything more gently and have a kinder demeanor, which comes from a kinder heart.

Focus on your potential instead of your
limitations.

Don't be paralyzed by the doubts that can permeate your mind before even setting out on your day. It's easy to do, and without conscious attention to it become a "runaway freight train." Having the courage it takes to work through the doubts is the key element to transcending your whole life, becoming the person you can be. Whether it's to be a success in business, a great athlete, or live a life of altruism, once you can continue to strive for what it is that is truly important to you, you'll be free to tap into all you have to offer the project. Easier said than done? Not really. There's no future in living in doubt, taking the pessimistic view, or living your life in fear. Having approached your days actively pursuing a goal, and more to the point, with unbridled *enthusiasm*, will make a mark on your days, and open your potential to myriad other avenues.

We're only human, and this "way of life," even for the most optimistic, "fortunate" of us, is not always easy. The "kinder, gentler" mentality that we can give back to the world more than we take is our choice to adopt and cease unwaveringly.

So many times in our day we have the opportunity to make a mark, however small, and raise the calibration of the world. Keeping these two simple, but impactful, concepts in mind can be the *deciding vote* in being less selfish, thinking outside ourselves, and taking a *kinder, gentler* approach. When we do so, we are instantly "lightened," and blood flows easier, through our entire bodies, and to our minds. We then become full-strength, to make the right decision, perform to our best physically, and heighten those around us.

Go get 'em: We do not inherit the land from our forefathers...we borrow it for our children.

"Contentment: Not the fulfillment of what you want, but the realization of how much you already have."

32

SERENITY

It doesn't take much to find true serenity. Being satisfied with what you have is the key. It's not that we shouldn't aspire to grow in our lives: our minds, our talents, our assets, but to be "at peace" with where we are right now, knowing we've given our best, while we aspire to "raise our game" is the true secret.

These are "must-do's" any given day; the path that leads to an inner solace that is hard to compare anything to. Not worldly goods.

> Laughter is not at all a bad beginning for a friendship, and it is far the best ending for one.
> — OSCAR WILDE

Laugh. It's physically and emotionally cleansing. You need to remember to laugh; the more you do so, the more it comes naturally, and you'll stop having to *try.* When you look at life with a "glass half-full" approach, things are easier to appreciate. Not to say everything's easy, but we're more willing to accept the opportunity that lies within a situation, albeit sometimes buried under the surface.

Breaking the ice with someone you'd like to know better, or just open lines of communication with, is seldom less labor-intensive than if introduced by laughter.

Sometimes nothing will propel us to tap our potential like adversity; a challenge that makes us toughen, commit, or "steel" ourselves to a goal. How do we do this? Start by getting outside our "comfort zone." The longer we stay, sometimes mired in the same mentality, we miss what's on "the other side of the curtain." It's easier to live our lives in a familiar range, risk-wise, and not take chances or tackle new endeavors. Why? Because it's the *unknown* most of us fear more than anything else. These are precisely the challenges that open new areas of our minds and show us talents we may not have dreamed we possess. These talents may be of a physical nature, but as often, they're the "intangibles," qualities that lie within us—stick-to-itiveness, character, compassion—and which awaken senses within us that bring us to our truer self.

Think. Challenge yourself. We all know what a rut is. We get locked into habits and responsibilities that have us programmed to simply *get to the end of the day.* This is understandable and sometimes necessary, but what is essential is that at some point, we *find a way* to divert from those habits. Whether it's writing a book, starting a running program, or devoting more time to family and less time to work, it takes a conscious effort to *resist staying stuck.*

What is it to be *stuck*? Simply put, it's not being willing to move on. If you want it enough, you can do it! Don't think of the entire project. Where you eventually want to be can feel daunting. Let nothing sabotage your getting started. Make it today. After all, what have we got to lose? Once the first and often most difficult step forward is taken, we immediately start to relax, and the momentum starts to flow.

English essayist Joseph Addison, who cofounded *The Spectator* magazine, had a great synopsis of what often results from opening our minds and an insight to the possibilities that lie beyond:

> Everything that is new or uncommon raises a pleasure in the imagination, because it fills the soul with an agreeable surprise, gratifies its curiosity, and gives it an idea of which it was not before possessed.
> — JOSEPH ADDISON

Feel deeply. Don't be afraid of emotion; to know you can feel that deeply reminds us of our humanity. It's sometimes the case that no matter how much optimism, drive, and stick-to-itiveness you have, nothing seems to be working. Whether referring to your professional goals, personal relationships, or athletic pursuits, it can at times feel as though you haven't made a good decision in months. Those are the times we find out what's truly important and indeed, what we're made of.

It's easy to be classy when everything's going well. What separates truly exceptional individuals, and those destined to make a difference, is staying in the game at a time like this. How do we best do this?

1) Devote a concerted amount of nonnegotiable time, daily or at least weekly, to the goal. Once you start, the *momentum* will keep you coming back
2) Don't think *results*, think *effort*. Some days you'll feel as if you didn't move forward, but like with an exercise program, each day you progress. The results don't come in a straight line, or predictably, but you have breakthroughs you can't even explain if you stick to your discipline
3) You always *empower* yourself when you take initiative.

> Never apologize for showing feeling. When you
> do so, you apologize for the truth.
> —BENJAMIN DISRAELI

> Don't cry because it's over. Smile because it
> happened.
> —DR. SEUSS

What you're going through is not terminal. Very seldom is it the case that what is causing you distress, pain, a "veering off course" from your goal is insurmountable. Once you realize this, a certain weight is lifted from your shoulders, and from there, you can operate full-strength toward whatever your goal may be. After all, the further "south" you feel things have gone, the more *upside* you have.

———————

Go get 'em: Be moved to tears. That way, you'll know you're still alive!

"Accept very selectively *criticism* and *compliments*."

33

MOVE FORWARD

Whatever it takes, keep positive momentum going.

As it's stated, if what you're doing now isn't working, "do the next right thing." This can be a small step forward, but that's the important thing: you're moving forward! You might have to endure criticism or even ridicule when enduring a rough patch, where nothing you do seems to bear fruit, as much as you believe in it. Don't sit still belaboring and embellishing how bad things are, or moreover, that life hasn't eventuated fairly or quite the way you drew it up. This only deepens the paralysis that can set in at times like this.

> "It is always with excitement that I wake up in the morning wondering what my intuition will toss up to me, like gifts from the sea. I work with it and rely on it. It's my partner."
> —JONAS SALK

Sometimes the smallest action that moves you in the right direction, starts you breathing normally, and leads to the next move forward is the springboard to bigger, more noteworthy breakthroughs. Also, each time you "rise to the occasion" like this, you become inherently stronger and more able to absorb the next issue that arises.

Go get 'em: Been down so long, it looks like up to me. Find the humor in the situation, and go from there!

"All the adversity I've had in my life, all my troubles and obstacles, have strengthened me... You may not realize it when it happens, but a kick in the teeth may be the best thing in the world for you."
—WALT DISNEY

34

ARCHITECT YOUR CHARACTER

Adversity is like having a root canal; you don't love the experience, but you probably wouldn't be going through it if you didn't need it!

Not only are patience, discipline, and persistence gained through outlasting adversity, but also there's an awakening of other senses. Gratitude, a change of focus, and a newfound appreciation of "the little things" are by-products of riding out these storms in our lives, whether little ones or seemingly life-changing ordeals. Additionally, even if life altering, there will be a tomorrow. This new day may find us emerging *stronger* and *exactly* where we were meant to be, though we never could have imagined this before being thrust into this "survival" mind-set. *Remember: To prevail is simple. Take just one more step when all others around you have quit.*

Go get 'em: There's no upside to quitting! Do the next "right" thing, and continue on while you wait for the results.

"Sometimes we are *forced* into directions we should have found ourselves..."

35

EVOLVE

Set into motion by the most surprising occurrences and at the most surprising times, our chance for growth emerges. In times of disappointment, trial, even despair, we are always just an act away from being the person we were meant to be.

> We cannot always do great things, but we can do small things with *great love*."
> —MOTHER TERESA

From a small act of kindness or altruism (or seemingly small at the time) can blossom a whole "way of life." An attitude of "assisting the world" in whatever manner able immediately pays us back. Our disposition lightens, problems are minimized, and we see the world through clearer, more appreciative eyes.

It becomes evident with abundance that our worries are, while still pertinent and necessary to own up to, relatively small compared to what most face. Also, we learn that when we give back to the world and "raise" its calibration we're magically elevated, and all our strivings, our challenges, and in fact, *our lives* become lighter.

Change is almost never welcomed. Even when we're not happy where we are, the uneasiness of major change is more powerful than the will to make the necessary moves.

Go get 'em: "There is but one pursuit in life which it is in the power of all to follow, and of all to attain. It is subject to no disappointments, since he that perseveres makes every difficulty an advancement, and every contest a victory; and this is the pursuit of virtue." —Charles Caleb Colton

"It's easy to be classy when everything's going right; how we deal with adversity puts our signature on the project…"

36

HUMILITY: NEGATIVES TO POSITIVES

Go to your strength, your passion, what drives you, what you do best. It's time to call upon *these* things to rekindle the fire that makes you "the best you can be." At these pivotal moments, making a life-altering decision can produce a paralyzing feeling we must get beyond in order to change what needs be changed. However testing it can be, these are the moments to remember:

> The fear won't help you save what you have, but
> it might make you lose what you can become...

For me, running is that passion that raises the level of my game, makes me the best I can be. I've faced a personal test in this area though, an injury that has required two surgeries, the latter a hip replacement. What I've gained from this misfortune far outreaches what I may have sacrificed during this time. Before going through it, though, I would have only been able to label this experience as "traumatic." I was always a "grateful" runner. Returning to the sport after this twist of fate has raised my appreciation for it to a new level.

While I may not have always gotten what I hoped for from the sport, the lessons gained along the way are precisely what allowed me to thrive and *grow* without it. Find your "sport" that lifts you to personal heights, whether it be something physical or a different kind of passion. It is all your own—cultivated, nurtured, and interpreted differently than by anyone else.

Go get 'em: "Enthusiasm is one of the most powerful engines of success. When you do a thing, do it with all your might. Put

your whole soul into it. Stamp it with your own personality. Be active, be energetic and faithful, and you will accomplish your object. Nothing great was ever achieved without enthusiasm."
—Ralph Waldo Emerson

"Success is not to be pursued; it is to be attracted by the person you become."
— JIM ROHN

37

POSSIBILITIES

By no means is every moment a picnic or easy. Nor was the next move in my quest to return to the sport always predictable. I run when I know I shouldn't, and the activities I "pinch-hit" with are sometimes a challenge and less gratifying. Yet those lessons of stick-to-itiveness, faith, and gratitude for what *can* be achieved sometimes lend gratification I wouldn't have been able to envision before my injury.

There is a great art in accepting that you can deal with pain by *being present in the moment,* just as it is, when it arises. Make no mistake: I don't condone working through physical pain without listening to the body and dealing accordingly with the decision of whether to lay off or work through it. With this mindfulness—and trusting our knowledge, senses, and instincts—we can make peace with pain. This includes not fearing that it will fail to get better. By doing this we do not allow opening of the door of dread as to what tomorrow will bring. Not always, but often, pain can be broken down to a temporary, less invasive feeling.

Bodily pain comes in many guises; some of it chronic, some temporary, some unavoidable. There are numerous strategies to ward pain off; avoiding it, seeing ourselves as victims, or taking it out on others, which only promotes agitation. Sometimes, we even camouflage it with distraction. When we let fear enter the equation and resistance to what we're feeling, there is little space for healing or "compassionate attention" to occur. Alternately, when we accept it as temporary (not denial or attempting to make it better, but *accepting* this is how it is right now) we "exhale" and usually find a sense of relief through dealing with how we feel and not through denial, which only causes it to linger.

Go get 'em: "One can't sail new oceans unless willing to lose sight of the shore…"

"Excellence…to do a common thing in an uncommon way."
— BOOKER T. WASHINGTON

38

VICTORY

When working toward a goal, one can look upon their pursuit as one that takes unusual courage or character, but the springboard really is *action*. In fact, striving and moving toward this goal is often more effectively accomplished with a more simplistic plan and one not so mentally daunting to undertake. A process of "staying the course" by taking small steps toward one's goal, not vastly changing the dynamics of our everyday lives, usually reaps more noticeable improvements. An added benefit is that they're more *sustainable* in nature, as our expectations are not that we'll travel the course by tomorrow. Instead, our entire psyche is shifted to a "kinder, gentler" approach, which activates the characteristics that reward us simply by their presence: gratitude, empathy, and overall empathy.

Our daily outlook sets the stage for the way we accomplish and accept things. The pride we take in how we treat people, approach responsibilities, and comport ourselves is most noticeably shaped not by grandiose acts, which have their place, but the self-respect we develop. This has us poised, indeed, *trains us* to not only act with dignity and lend quality to what others take note of. Instead, it implores us to approach life with an ingrained *integrity* no one can take away from us, even when not noticed. By the way, at some point it *will* be taken account of.

Go get 'em: Write down one thing you'd like to accomplish today—then do it.

"Nobody can make you feel inferior without your consent."
— ELEANOR ROOSEVELT

39

SELF-CONFIDENCE

For many of us, self-confidence seems self-evident. If you feel self-confident, you don't often doubt your own abilities. Yet if you're not confident, it's hard to let go of worry about a myriad of things, like how others perceive you.

For teachers, self-confidence creates a unique challenge. It's important to convey a sense of confidence, but how should that self-confidence manifest itself? Display too much, and it comes across as self-importance. Display too little, and your students' trust in your abilities might wane.

Go get 'em: As a mentor, leave your imprint on people. You can do it in a number of ways, and there's very little more important that you can do in this world.

"Go to your strength."

40

BELIEVE

Now what is self-confidence?

To do what you do well and not think too much about how others perceive you.

Achieving self-confidence poses different challenges. If you're less experienced in showing your abilities, you usually feel more concerned about the perception of others. You're still finding your path.

We get thrown off when we focus, though, on one negative reaction, when we may have been greeted by ten positives.

That's okay. It's human nature for that one negative comment to stick, even when so strongly outnumbered by approval. We wake up each day for acceptance, to gain approval, and to be given positive feedback.

The irony is that to build self-confidence, we have to let go of the need to be seen as confident, to always have our actions outwardly affirmed. Pride is involved here, and while this doesn't mean we should disregard our reputation, quite the contrary, we should stay focused when we feel we're on the right path, and if met with questioning not yield to popular opinion.

By doing so—and it doesn't have to be through boisterous attention-gathering—you show resilience. Sometimes the more understated one is, the more notice comes one's way.

You're not responsible for making sure it is perfect for everyone. Spreading joy is about setting an example, not telling people what to do.

After Grete Waitz won her first of nine New York City marathons, she stated, "I'm not going to run this again." Emotions ran high, and after things calmed, she looked at things through more reasoned, less emotional glasses. The results speak for themselves.

Go get 'em: Be unstoppable. If you want it enough, feel its toughness, but never relinquish the dream.

"It's good we all don't think the same…if we did, we'd all love my wife."
— WILLIAM HOWELL

41

TRANQUILITY

Recognizing your limits is crucial to building self-confidence. Be secure in the knowledge that you have but also okay with not always knowing the answer.

Be prepared.

Don't belabor your mistakes.

Meet your destination face-to-face.

Have a life away from your pursuit.

Be able to get outside yourself, and don't be one-dimensional. When you take a break, you take a breath, and you come back to your passion more ready than ever to "raise your game."

Own it

Be fully responsible for your actions. "Not 'I'm doing this because my teacher said to,' but 'I own this, I'm doing it because it makes sense to me.' Having a sense of ownership gives you that sense of self-confidence."

Don't be someone else's imitation; be your own original.

Everyone has a gift that forms his or her own legacy. Find yours, and let it out *every day* in some way. If it's the ability to make people feel good, appreciate it, and bring it out. You owe it to the world, and not only others, but *you* will be rewarded in a plethora of ways.

Go for it: Enjoy what you do. Then you'll do it well and be a success.

"I can't imagine a person becoming a success who doesn't give this game of life everything he's got."
— WALTER CRONKITE

42

GOOD ENOUGH

This doesn't mean that sometimes, after "fighting the good fight," we shouldn't steer our efforts toward another direction. What I speak to here is that the goal can change, sometimes without our even knowing so.

Once you "steel" yourself to your mission, no matter what you confront, you can take *victory* from never relinquishing the "striving" toward a better place in life, a higher goal, a better outcome. Even if your goal doesn't eventuate as you first drew it up, the inner strength that can be attained from sheer *stick-to-itiveness* creates new and sometimes more long-standing gratification.

Build on your accomplishments: Halfway through the long run (or major life project), assess things, realize what you've gotten done, and instead of mentally laboring over what remains—which wastes energy, time, and enthusiasm—this momentum of accomplishment becomes incentive for your finishing the goal with fervor.

> No matter how busy you may think you are, you
> must find time for reading, or surrender yourself
> to self-chosen ignorance.

An important point is to not become overwhelmed with what lies before you; take breaks. Make them structured, in duration and intermittency, but be sure you take them.

It's quality of time spent, not usually quantity. This extends to your time with family and interpersonal relationships, not only work projects, workout regimen, and "to-do" lists. Have you ever experienced embarking upon a project and hours later seemingly nothing had gotten done? Have the wherewithal to gauge what you're accomplishing, and if it's not your day to apply focus where you've started, redirect that effort and time toward a path that elicits a positive response, an immediate gratification of sorts, and watch the momentum build. Be present with your friends, family, children. It's hard to get that time back. We all have responsibilities that threaten our time, so make it count!

Go get 'em: "Many people will walk in and out of your life, but only true friends will leave footprints in your heart." —Eleanor Roosevelt

"Art begins in imitation and ends in innovation."
— MASON COOLEY,
American aphorist

43

PRACTICE

Practice always involves seeing our edge and taking a small step beyond it into the unknown. As a Spanish proverb says, "If you do not dare, you do not live." Nietzsche echoed this when he said, "The secret of the greatest fruitfulness and the greatest enjoyment of existence is: to live dangerously!" The premise here is not necessarily talking about doing physically dangerous things; I'm not in favor of that approach. What it speaks to is taking a step beyond our edge of comfort.

Still, we have to step toward our edge by ourselves. Instead of regarding our edge as an enemy, a place we prefer to avoid, we can realize that our edge is actually *our path*. From this place, we begin to explore more clearly what we're really made of. However, we can do this only one step at a time, persevering through all the ups and downs of our lives. We don't have to leap in headfirst, going for all or nothing. In fact, rarely is that constructive. We can simply take a small step, supported by the knowledge that everyone feels fear in stepping beyond the illusion of comfort.

Go get 'em: Promise to think only of the best, to work only for the best, and to expect only the best in yourself and others.

"You gain strength, courage, and confidence by every experience in which you really stop to look fear in the face. You must do the thing which you think you cannot do."
—ELEANOR ROOSEVELT

44

PERFECT PRACTICE

The real measure of practice is whether, little by little, we can find our edge. That place may even entail fear, as we go where we've not been before. This is where winners are separated; they allow themselves to experience it. This takes courage, but courage isn't about becoming fearless. *Courage is the willingness to experience our fears.* And as we experience our fears, courage grows. Noticing our edge and trying to meet it also allows us to develop compassion, not just for ourselves but for the whole human drama. Then, with an increasing sense of lightness and curiosity, we can keep moving toward a more open and genuine life.

Go get 'em: Prepare so well that you get the most out of yourself at moments of great pressure.

"Pressure is simply the task at hand exceeding our level of preparation."

45

PATTERNS

All patterns represent order. When we leave an old pattern behind, we enter a liminal space. Like the space between an exhalation and the next inhalation, this place is ripe with unlimited possibilities for new choices.

This in-between space can be unsettling. During a recent session, a woman poignantly asked, "If I let go of these beliefs, will I still be myself?" We often resist new patterns for fear of losing the identities we've so carefully constructed. Yet it's true that when we change a long-held pattern, we undergo a rebirth of sorts.

Samskara, a term used in yoga practice, is defined as a perfecting and polishing, a process of cultivation. Improving our samskara brings us closer to our true nature, which is the goal of yoga. Applying to life in general, then shifting samskara is the ongoing work of chipping away at our negative patterns to illuminate our positives.

Changing daily actions in a way that promotes confidence and happiness promotes *positive momentum*, which we then build upon. Like alchemists in our own transformation, we do have the capacity to constantly refine and direct our actions and thoughts into healthier designs.

When we experience a step back, which is inevitable, we "climb back on the horse." How many people, famous and otherwise, with goals and dreams have derailed numerous times, have met success through perseverance, and as important, a "never-say-die" resilience, which is born from a mind-set as much so as from an action.

Our greatest glory is not in never falling, but in getting up every time we do.
—CONFUCIUS

The good news is that the ability to shift our patterns—once we've sown the seeds—is self-generating, self-sustaining, and self-renewing. When we're patient enough to accept it, to honor its inner sound and slow rhythm, *change* simply flows. And it's a joy to taste the reward of all this hard work in its natural form, the sweetness that arises from seeing long labor and preparation come to fruition.

It's easy to have faith in yourself and have discipline when you're a winner, when you're number one. What you got to have is faith and discipline when you're not a winner.
—VINCE LOMBARDI

The words "finish strong" instantly and clearly communicate a performance goal perhaps better than any other two words in our language.

This mind-set is not limited to the athletic arena. You can incorporate it into your personal and professional life, meaning as much to ultimate fulfillment as any other talent or trait you bring to the table.

Go get 'em: Find a positive when you get up in the morning, and go for it! Just one thing: physical, mental, or emotional. This sets your mind positively, builds adrenalin, and establishes momentum.

"To be able at any moment to sacrifice what we are for what we could become; that is *courage*."

—CHARLES DUBOIS

46

NIMBLE

We're not talking about being quick and agile here, though that never hurts. To be nimble, actionwise, means not waiting for all your ducks to be in a row—instead, having the courage, presence under pressure, and sometimes just the intestinal fortitude to *act*!

When you expect all the stars to align perfectly before making a move that can enhance your life or someone else's, you risk losing an opportunity that can bring you closer to what you're mourning having lost. In other words, when we allow past disappointments or bad breaks to stranglehold us, we're paralyzed from acting to move unless we own where we are presently, knowing it's not where we'll stay. This literally frees us and brings us much closer to the very success we strived for initially. We seek respect and honor from achievements, our image of success, or how we're perceived. We often only realize these from the way we deal with adversity.

Go get 'em: "Start by doing what's necessary; then do what's possible; and suddenly you are doing the impossible." —St. Francis of Assisi

"Never doubt that a small group of thoughtful, committed people can change the world. Indeed it is the only thing that ever has."
— MARGARET MEAD

47

FOCUS

Goals, events, *results* are sometimes are visualized so easily in our mind's eye. Yet something keeps us from pursuing, or once immersed, finishing as strongly as we can. Picture a six-mile run; you're fatigued and have only a quarter-mile left. That short distance at that point can seem daunting. Instead of thinking of how tired you are, or the task at hand, *break it down*. Garner energy from the success you've already achieved; think of those two minutes remaining in terms of four thirty-second excerpts, and as you whittle them down, you find yourself *more* energized and able to not only finish, but with vigor. In this way, the mind and all its best traits: *positive attitude, sense of accomplishment,* and *gratitude* have all entered the experience and worked for you, as they always do. We simply must call upon these traits. All of us possess them. You might even package them together to define a grander state: that of *enlightenment*.

Go get 'em: When things get tough, think of how far you've come, not how far you have to go.

"Everyone sees the unseen in proportion to the clarity of one's heart, and that depends upon how much one has polished it..."

48

VISION

Yogis tend to agree that in a sense we all are enlightened; we are *already there*. Enlightenment is really a deep, basic trust in yourself, that in your own way, you have the ability to better the world. You must have the desire, too.

We display an enlightened state by exhibiting the self-confidence to listen and be quiet...simply letting our positive influence raise the level of the environment we're in. The work that awaits us is stripping away the layers of self-doubt, or *distraction*, that we have accumulated, so that our natural state of peace and wholeness can be revealed.

> "It is not what we get but who we become, what
> we contribute...that gives meaning to our lives."
> —ANTHONY ROBBINS

In other words, we've always had it within our being.

Enlightenment is not a new state that is in any way obtained or achieved. It more accurately entails the uncovering of our original nature that has always been present.

Thinking yourself into an enlightened state is a particularly clever way of countering the negative tendencies of the mind. The root cause of fear or anger or addiction is the feeling of being alone or isolated and separate from everything else. Any moment you can shift that viewpoint, you eliminate a layer or two of fear and anger. The more you can do that, the more you shift the neuronal pathways that create all the "enemies" of your happiness.

Practicing enlightenment is sometimes a sophisticated

exercise in: "doing what it takes." Of course, it works only when you do it for its own sake, not because you're trying to impress people and definitely not to claim a mastery you don't possess. You do it for the same reason kids pretend to do grown-up things—because it habituates you to the mature self you will one day become.

You alone are in control of your happiness. Like any discipline, if you want it enough, and practice, you perfect it. Also, like a coach, you can spread it to others and around the world.

———————

Go get 'em:
> Looking back it seems to me,
> All the grief that had to be
> Left me when the pain was o'er
> Stronger than I was before.

"They must often change, who would be constant in happiness or wisdom."
— CONFUCIUS

49

CALIBRATE HIGHER

Whether out of necessity or not, *change* is to be expected. While that's often not the case, what we can control about change and its outcome is in the art of *embracing* it. That is an art form that we cultivate through experience, a mentality of *grace* when the unexpected (which more often than not is how change greets us) comes along.

"Life's a marathon, not a sprint."

If you're on the right track but it seems progress isn't coming fast enough, call upon your patience—stay the course. Very little of note comes quickly when speaking of success or breakthroughs.

The only reason we really pursue goals is to cause ourselves to expand and grow. Achieving goals by themselves will never make us happy in the long term. It's the person we evolve into through overcoming obstacles along the way.

The human mind is far more fertile, far more incredible and mysterious than the land, but it works the same way. It doesn't care what we plant...success or failure. A concrete, worthwhile goal *or* confusion, misunderstanding, fear, anxiety, and so on. What we plant must return to us. It's the same with *attitude*; one who consistently thinks positively will have clarity, vision, and stick-to-itiveness in heightened proportion, and chances are, will see things through to their goal.

Go get 'em: Be nimble of body and mind. When you set a good example, you raise the bar for everyone around you.

"I've missed more than 9,000 shots in my career. I've lost almost 300 games. Twenty-six times, I've been trusted to take the game winning shot and missed. I've failed over and over and over again in my life. And that is why I succeed."
— MICHAEL JORDAN

50

ARE YOU KIDDING ME?

Look to a shrub with small dark red blossoms on it and note that if you give the plant too much water it doesn't bloom. It thrives and blossoms under just the right amount of environmental stress.

It reminds me of another story of a butterfly, perched on a windowsill, struggling to escape its cocoon. A helpful observer, watching its struggle, decides to gently cut the creature's cocoon open and free it. When the wet butterfly finally emerges, it's unable to fly because what was intended to be helpful had actually prevented the butterfly from strengthening its wings to prepare it for flight.

Perhaps the stress we experience can be a presage of beautiful flowers or elegant flight in our own lives. Perhaps if we are patient and stop to be grateful for our experiences, we too, like the plant or the butterfly, will blossom or fly in unexpected ways as a result of the stress, rather than being defeated by it.

I don't mean we should seek to find stress. I am saying, from firsthand experience, that's it's not always a bad thing. We need the right amount of tension to keep us "blossoming." While we humans are more complex than plants, we can learn valuable lessons by observing nature.

If you're in a period when stress seems to be your constant companion, take a lesson from nature.

Instead of asking, "Why am I having to deal with all of this?" ask yourself what you most need to learn from your experiences. View the situation much like the butterfly must see its cocoon, as a barrier you must break through to become the extraordinary creature you were designed to be.

It's not always easy to maintain such a perspective. We often make our experiences harder than they have to be by our resistance to change, growth, or stress. Stay focused and use stress to take you a step closer to the flower or butterfly you want to become.

> It is a basic principle of spiritual life that we learn the deepest things in unknown territory. Often it's when we feel most confused inwardly and are in the midst of our greatest difficulties that something new will open. We awaken most easily to the mystery of life through our weakest side. The areas of our greatest strength, where we are the most competent and clearest, tend to keep us away from the mystery.

Go get 'em: Sometimes you've just gotta say, "What next?" and throw up your hands. Know, then, this too will pass.

PART THREE
PART THREE
PART THREE
PART THREE

OL' MO

"We can only be said to be alive in those moments when our hearts are conscious of our treasures."
— THORNTON WILDER

51

OLYMPIC

External pressures can paralyze us and actually lead to negative performance. Think of the Olympics creed:

> The most important thing is not to win, but to take part, just as the most important thing in life is not the triumph but the struggle. The essential thing is not to have conquered, but to have fought well.

As well, the Special Olympics creed speaks to this principle:

> Let me win, but if I can not win, let me be brave in the attempt.

Very powerful, and all you have to know. It embodies giving our best effort, but more to the point, all the courage, steadfastness, and *will* to stay the course, against factors out of our control and above odds that seem unbeatable.

> Life isn't about how to survive the storm, *but how to dance in the rain.*

Winning is not it; we can't control our opposition or inevitabilities that may arise. What we *can* affect daily is our willingness to keep striving, which is the true accomplishment.

Have you noticed the unadulterated joy with which Special Olympians take part in their sport? Even before they splash into the pool, take their lanes on the track, or prepare to lift the barbell, they're unabashedly thrilled to be participating. It's a great lesson to learn. Some clutter their minds and days to a point where forgotten is the fact that it's all about *being in the game* and how fortunate we are to have our destiny in our own hands. We can always find positives in our situation, our day... our lives. We've just got to look, and think.

Go get 'em: Everything has a second act and a third act. Everybody gets to write his or her own endings.

"Live not as though there were a thousand years ahead of you. Fate is at your elbow; make yourself good while life and power are still yours."
— MARCUS AURELIUS

52

STRIVE

It's not always easy to bound out of the starting gates each morning with renewed zeal for the day to come. Maybe you didn't have a full night's sleep or get enough quality from the night's rest. A dilemma, worry, or even a work project may be on your mind that "weighs" you down and "paralyzes" you from getting a solid start on the day. Don't give up on the day. In fact, make it a challenge to conquer it!

There's a sure-fire way to kick-start things, and while no guarantees exist as to where the day takes you, it gives you the best chance I know to build adrenalin and just maybe *put your signature* on the day.

It's about *momentum*. Find that *positive action* that gets you going. It can be reading, meditating, doing yoga, or just a few floor exercises. Five minutes can set your energy force in motion. This will trigger a positive mind-set from which to build upon. The first step is the toughest, but the gratification from it will pay you back in multiples.

Go get 'em: Experience success first thing. Everything becomes easier.

"I felt like I played in a very rough football game
with no hitting above the waist."
— ALAN PAGE,
NFL hall-of-famer
commenting on running a marathon

53

ASPIRE

In the pursuit of doing well by others, you need not compromise your aspirations. In fact, your own successes—and what it takes to get there—create the springboard for giving back to the world.

An unwavering vision to run a marathon, for instance, gives you a fifty percent greater chance of bringing this goal to fruition. This pursuit can be envisioned without any "caveats." I have to run it in a certain time-frame, I have to *run* the whole thing without walking, etc. Purely and simply: I will finish a marathon!

Also, this is a perfect example of a goal that should be undertaken for no other reason—or no one else's desires—other than personal. The mental "workload" involved in trying to please, compete with, or impress others only drains and distracts us from our singular pursuit. Do it for the right reasons. Other missions should certainly be strived for altruistically, but remember the balance. As the Hebrew saying goes, *"If I'm not for myself, who will be for me? If I'm only for myself, what good am I?"* That path that nurtures you and makes you the best you can be, transcending yourself, is a fair and noble road.

If you have a clear goal and a plan to achieve it, your focus is fixed on a set course of action. Instead of becoming sidetracked by distractions and diversions, your time is focused on a straight line from start to finish.

1) Character: Treat others as you want to be treated.
2) Integrity: Whatever you aspire to, live up to your standards, whether *anyone's watching* or not.

3) Vision: See what is worth aspiring to, and don't lose focus.
4) Money: Spending and saving—a balancing act.

Studies show that under 5 percent of adults have written goals and plans, and they earn more than the other 97 percent put together. I don't think this comparison pertains only to money, but to accomplishment in general. Income, though, is a tangible marker that can be measured. It's okay and sometimes necessary to aspire to specific monetary goals. Also, this is a great springboard to the next step. Other more altruistic goals that raise the "calibration of the world."

5) Compassion: Don't miss an opportunity to lend to someone's life; you may never know the change you affect.

————

Go get 'em: Do you have these characteristics in proper perspective? It takes an investment of time, discipline, and dedication, but it's worth it.

"When nothing seems to help, I go and look at a stonecutter hammering away at his rock, perhaps a hundred times without as much as a crack showing in it. Yet at the hundred and first blow it will split in two, and I know it was not that last blow that did it, but all that had gone before."
— JACOB A. RIIS

54

WHAT HAVE YOU GOT?

Self-discipline is more important than talent. It's usually acquired through persistence, not a birthright, so it's more likely cultivated and called upon inherently when needed. It balks at laziness, builds resilience as the task deepens, and won't take *no* for an answer.

"If you don't know where you're going, any road will get you there."

Why is this? The simplest answer? This is why people with goals accomplish so much more than people without them.

Applying discipline to all these aspects of life sets you apart from the masses. It pertains to:

> "You miss every shot you don't take."
> —WAYNE GRETZKY

1) Something (things) must drive us. Think of it this way: you can't hit a target you can't see.
2) Time management: Be self-driven.
3) Personal fitness: To be on top of our game, we must respect our health.

The desire for external wealth is not evil. In fact, it's innate to humans. When the intensity of these longings becomes skewed, it can cause unhappiness on both a practical level and a spiritual one. In order to afford things, you have to work long hours, leaving you less time for what truly sustains you, whether that's yoga and meditation, a hobby, or time with your kids. An expensive lifestyle also limits your choice of career, forcing you to take a high-paying job that may not be fulfilling.

It's hard to transcend the desire for external things when we see hundreds of ads implying that happiness lies in a new iPod, laptop, or car. Yet despite those commercial messages, acquisition doesn't equal happiness.

Finding a balance that transcends our craving for *more* can lead to fulfilling, more satisfying, albeit more modest lives. You may ask how we then can give back when we have potentially less of a well to draw from? The answer lies in the myriad of examples seen where people of lesser means contribute dramatically to humanity…by adoption, Big Brothers Big Sisters, and other such worthy organizations. We can usually do this with the resources at hand, without waiting for material abundance. These are gifts of their time, compassion, and heart—not only their assets.

Go get 'em: Be driven, but always strive for balance in life.

"We are the world, we are the children, we are the ones who make a brighter day, so let's start giving."
—"WE ARE THE WORLD," 1985/2010

55

COMPETING: WHO'S REALLY THE OPPOSITION?

The great teacher and mentor and, yes, also famed basketball coach of the UCLA Bruins men's team, John Wooden, was widely known to never mention the team's opponent, or even watch film of them, when preparing for a game. He held to the notion that if you prepared to your fullest then the results would be taken care of accordingly.

He furthered this notion when discussing pursuits *outside* the athletic arena. This is why I came to see him as one of the great teachers our society has seen.

The material things we garner are only worthwhile, after we take care of our responsibilities, pursuant to what we do with them to better humanity—such as raise the calibration of the world around us, and by extension, the entire universe. We often *never know* how much effect we have on people, both when we act and after, and whom it is whose life will change by what we do. We *each* have that capacity!

An example of this is in my family business, the first pawn-shop opened in the state of Oklahoma. That was 1911, and my grandfather began the business that would span three generations and eighty-eight years.

This was a very hands-on, small business, and I'd like to think the "personal touch" we lent was the reason we knew roughly eight of every ten customers who came in. I was very grateful to work with my parents from the time I graduated college for nearly twenty-five years, and they taught me plenty. The greatest lesson was that you treat everyone the way you'd like to be treated, judging not their status or financial worth, but their underlying character. To this end, the greatest source of pride I took from that time in the family business, along with the enjoyment of working so closely with my parents, was the fact that today I still see a number of old customers, and we're always so pleased to run into each other. We sold the business years ago, and just recently, two former customers approached me to say hello. They didn't do so because they wanted to conduct business. Instead it was because of the way they were treated in our store...as a *person* and an *equal*. How you treat someone when you have the "upper hand" tells much about the measure of an individual. When you grant respect to someone who deserves it, yet isn't shown it on a regular basis, what it does for that person in terms of self-worth is often monumental.

Go get 'em: Lasting peace of mind doesn't come from what you accumulate. It is born from what you possess inside, and lend to others.

"True heroism is remarkably sober, very undramatic. It is not the urge to surpass all others at whatever cost, but the urge to serve others, at whatever cost."
— ARTHUR ASHE

56

ORDINARY MIRACLES

My father is in many ways a hero to me. He taught me many things, but at the top of the list, he taught me to live a life of example, not words. First and foremost, what he showed me was to treat people with respect, to live the Golden Rule. I remember one particular instance of him teaching this "life lesson" as if it were yesterday.

In my childhood years, my parents would let me work in the pawnshop that remained in my family for eighty-eight years, teaching me how to handle money and vital elements of owning a business. How to assess human nature and treat people accordingly were high on their list of traits to instill within me, and again, this was done largely *by example*, day in and day out.

You see, in the pawnshop setting, when a customer comes in to borrow money on their merchandise, the proprietor, it can be said, has the upper hand in that the customer needs you. We never looked upon it that way. Yet I've heard many examples from customers, many of whom became our friends, being taken advantage of by other store owners. Of course, there are honest and not-so-honest people in every business; I only speak from where I have experience. What I noticed about my dad was that he approached all our customers, no matter their socioeconomic placement, the same, with dignity and fairness. This is a characteristic I heard my grandfather who started the business had (he died when I was two). While my grandfather was outwardly warm and more talkative, my father did it in his own way, also in a soft-spoken manner, but with fewer words.

One afternoon I observed my dad talking to all the customers as they came in and conducting business as he usually did—methodically, but with a personal touch. At the end of the day, just as Dad was closing, a regular customer—one I knew—also came in.

I was ready to go home, and I thought that surely Dad, as he had worked a long day, wouldn't spend too much time with him, but I was wrong. Dad greeted him at the door with a welcome and asked about his family, most of whom had been in the store. He empathized with the man's hardships, listened to him as he obviously needed to tell someone what he was going through, and he didn't rush him once to get on with business. I kept looking at the clock, and when the man finally left, I asked, "Dad, why did you spend so much time with him? He just wanted to talk, and he'll be back. You could listen to his story anytime."

Dad then looked at me, locked the front door to the store, and said, "Let's talk, Mark."

He said, "I'm your father, and I've tried to teach you lots of things, as all fathers should. But if you remember nothing else I ever tell you, remember this: treat every human being just the way that you would want to be treated."

He said, "I know this is not the first time you've heard it, but I want to make sure it's the first time you *really* understand it, because if you had understood, you wouldn't have said what you did." We sat there and talked for another hour about the meaning and the power of the Golden Rule.

Dad said, "If you live the Golden Rule, everything else in life will usually work itself out, but if you don't, your life probably will be very unhappy, no matter what else you accomplish."

My favorite saying has now become "Treat others the way you want to be treated; the rest is merely color commentary." Translated: Live by the Golden Rule, and you'll have all the wealth you'll ever need. You'll have the respect of others, and an incalculable estate, in the form of peace of mind. Dad taught, and more valuably showed me the Golden Rule, and I only hope by my actions that I've made him proud.

———————————

Go get 'em: Do someone a favor today, even if they haven't asked for it.

"If you add a little to a little, and then do it again, soon that little shall be much."
—GREEK POET HESIOD

57

PROGRESS

Goal: See yourself where you want to be. Lose fifty pounds, become a runner, get to the Olympic marathon trials. Realize it won't happen tomorrow and that this *process* is actually where your personal growth materializes. The goal is simply gravy.

Get started: Effort actually breeds strength; the more you work, the more you attain confidence, stick-to-itiveness.

Gains: Measure progress weekly, but it won't be "linear." Every week you won't notice the same success toward goal, so don't beat yourself up. If you're staying true to the game plan, it will come. As you progress, you must prepare for *diminishing returns,* as you can't humanly continue losing ten pounds every two weeks, running two minutes faster every 10K, or experiencing noticeable gains in personal growth every week. The cumulative effect and attention to perseverance will manifest in time.

Gratification: Look at gains you make as "mini-victories." It's not all about a single goal, but an enhanced "way of life." We don't have to wear it on our sleeves. Even our closest friends and family don't want to hear that all the time. This doesn't preclude us from accepting and being thankful for positive changes in our life.

Goal: The yoga practice in which you use your mind and imagination to create an inner experience, to contemplate an enlightened reaction to an object of desire, say, or to an obstacle to overcome. The idea is that by using your mind to hold enlightened ideas and using your imagination to "pretend" enlightenment, you begin to create an inner experience of these states.

Get started: Once you do, no matter what you confront, you can take *victory* from never relinquishing the "striving" toward a better place in life, a higher goal...put simply, a better outcome. *That's* the victory!

Gains: When success becomes less "noticeable," this is actually good. It means you're adapting to the new *you*; you're fitter, more intact, whatever your aim. You've arrived! Therefore you won't see such quick, drastic changes as you did at the start. Taking the place of that outward change is something even *more* powerful—your newly found feeling of self-assuredness that you are constantly moving toward the place you want to be.

Grit: There *will* be "peaks and valleys" in any pursuit of betterment. In a marathon, very rarely does the day go without a glitch. You've taken the leap of faith in beginning, so embrace this temporary adversity. Stress is not a bad thing; it's the way we progress. You've done the work, so relax, call upon your conditioning and mental preparation, and know you'll ride the tough times out. It's about *confidence*.

Through these principles, we seek *gratification*. Peace of mind, however, is really our goal. This pursuit can take on many faces, and what road we travel is purely our choice.

Go get 'em: It all boils down to stick-to-itiveness, in relationships, athletic pursuits, or becoming the person you want to be. If you have unwavering dedication, you'll find success.

"Be the person your dog thinks you are."

58

ASPIRE—BUT TO *WHAT?*

If you don't have integrity, you have nothing. You can't buy it, and you might have all the money in the world, but if you are not a moral and ethical person, you really have nothing.

In the Indian tradition, life is said to have four aims—wealth, pleasure, ethical conduct or goodness, and enlightenment—and they are meant to be held in balance. What would your life be like if you were to cultivate each of these areas equally?

Wealth. Resources that sustain your life: skills, education, job, money, housing, food, clothing.

Pleasure. Every form of healthy enjoyment: sports, theater, literature, music, and art; practicing your own form of creative expression.

Ethical conduct. Earning a living honestly, taking care of responsibilities, acting morally, and according to your highest values. Helping others.

Enlightenment. Realizing your deepest nature; an inner "calm." Pursuing practices such as yoga, meditation, and spiritual study to make this possible. What we're really talking about is *peace of mind.*

Go get 'em: When you've done your best, *relax.* Then keep doing your best.

"Chance favors those in motion."
—JAMES H. AUSTIN

59

PLAY

Physical challenge covers a wide range of situations. Following are a few basic guidelines that can be used in many or most circumstances:

1) *Focus* on what you can do, even if there is no physical movement possible. Just the act of visualization has many benefits. Kinesthetic visualization (imagining body movement) has therapeutic benefits that have been well documented by scientific study and research.

2) *Relax.* Slow, relaxed movement like stretching or T'ai Chi engages a different part of the nervous system than more vigorous exercise does. T'ai Chi, or similar exercises, often help open blocks in the meridians (energy channels), blood vessels, and nerves, according to traditional Chinese medicine. Many injuries, traumas, or illnesses cause blocks that can thus be worked out and relieved.

3) *Center.* When we talk about "centering" this point is related to the body's center of gravity. Focusing on this point helps with balance and coordination, empowering the movement, and facilitating greater ease of motion.

3) *Ground.* Grounding, rooting, and sinking refer to several interconnected aspects of T'ai Chi practice. Grounding, as in the electrical system of your house, helps to dissipate excessive energy. It often relates to the alignment of the body as well, helping it to root in a good stance. Sinking (Soong) relates to letting go of tension, like surrendering to gravity. As an example, think of holding up a heavy object and letting it drop. "Soong" involves letting it drop, releasing tension, and

relaxing. Like the previously mentioned basics, grounding, rooting, and sinking are all interdependent and interconnected, and help us achieve mental—as well as physical—calm.

A small movement is better than none. Both in terms of technique and sheer effort, take a realistic approach to goals. The fact we don't get there immediately validates that what we're striving for is worth it, like the adage "anything worth doing takes time." Also, we may not always know the course we'll take. Once you've established that it's worth striving for, "fake it 'til you make it." Many students who cannot yet do something in the same way as their teacher or coach does just give up. The teacher is the teacher for a reason. Teachers do not become experts by giving up. They would rather see you push, try, and fail, than quit.

Go get 'em: Exercise is essential, as much for the mind as the body. It's not to do *a lot* seldom; instead, do *something* often.

"Care, admitted as guest, quickly turns to be master."

60

INTEGRITY

Why are some people more successful than others? Why do some people make more money, live happier lives, and accomplish much more in the same number of years than the great majority?

My whole life I've considered myself one of the *very* luckiest people around. Part of that view comes, I'm certain, from my mother's ingrained optimism. It surely rubbed off. Still, I began asking, "Why are some people more successful than others?" This question changed my life.

Over the years, I've tried to take note of various approaches to this question, whether via athletes I've spoken to or chronicled, or articles and books read on the subjects of success and achievement. As you're no doubt aware, every possible angle to this subject has been articulated upon and in every conceivable way.

The difference lies in how much you care, your inherent integrity. This translates to your treatment of others and can't be faked, at least not for long.

The power of study, prayer, even yoga and consistent exercise have been cited as keys to raising one's game, being the best you can be. All of these approaches are valid, but if one "magic bullet" exists that offers the closest thing to a *guarantee* of success, and I'm talking overall success, it would be what I call *stick-to-itiveness*.

Go get 'em: Be more concerned with character than reputation. Reputation is just what others think of you. You can't always control that. Character is ingrained, of which you are the sole owner.

"They don't care how much you know until they know how much you care."

61

CARE DEEPLY OR DON'T BOTHER

One might instantly ask, "Why stick-to-itiveness and not *compassion, humility,* or *altruism?*" That's easy to explain! This truly great personal quality, when it becomes habit or "way of life," draws all these others into active duty and instills the seminal quality we must call upon to accomplish a "life well lived" ... *personal accountability.*

It cannot be bought, and seldom is taught. It comes first and foremost from a desire down deep, which can be encapsulated in one statement: Do *all* you can, *when* you should, whether you *feel like it* or not!

———————————

Go get 'em: "The only real failure in life is not to be true to the best one knows."—Buddha

"The one who moved a mountain was the one who began carrying away the small stones."
— CHINESE PROVERB

62

LOOKING FOR OL' "MO"

There are two types of *momentum* that we experience—negative and positive. When you're having a rough time physically or emotionally, you must ride out the waves of hopelessness. They threaten your foundation. First step in conquering these thoughts is to ask yourself: is it terminal? Almost always this takes a load off your mind, as you mentally view a "worse-case" scenario and realize whatever you're confronting is not that bad. You're hurting midway through a marathon, your day isn't going as you would have hoped, there's a guy in front of you who doesn't see the light turn green. Take a breath; this too will pass. And every time you face such "roadblocks" with a "kinder, gentler" approach, you strengthen your resilience to the next such occurrence. This works with major life experiences as well as more mundane events, and this reframed attitude builds upon itself, as you slowly begin navigating your day with a brighter, more upbeat backdrop.

Go get 'em: You may not make your impact by being the most talented or inherently smartest. You're assured to, though, by being the most diligent of effort.

"A positive attitude may not solve all your problems, but it will annoy enough people to make it worth the effort."
— HERM ALBRIGHT

63

FLOW

The truth is, you hold within yourself a template for enlighten-ment. Whether you call it an "attitude of gratitude," there is at your core something, an essence that is effortless, joyous, and free.

Conditions, as well as *life,* are fluid, and they *will* change. With optimism, faith, and stick-to-itiveness, your chances for positive momentum are enhanced immeasurably.

Without a plan, albeit nimble enough to change to meet new developments, these aforementioned traits are hollow. The plan can be meticulous in nature or general.

Go get 'em: The glass is either half-empty or three-quarters full. You get to choose.

"Don't be afraid to go out on a limb. That's where the fruit is."
—H. JACKSON BROWN

64

PROSPERITY

Do you tend to see your life as half empty or half full? Do you struggle to get by, or do you generally get your needs met? Do you see the shortcomings of people or situations first or the pure potential? The answers to these questions may serve as your prosperity barometer.

To move from a state of struggle to a state of effortless grace, you'll need to cultivate prosperity consciousness.

1. Set your intention for what you desire and know that you deserve it.
2. Release any scarcity mentality and trust that you will be provided for.
3. Feel gratitude for what you have, rather than desire for what others have, or what you do not.

Go get 'em: Build momentum by being focused, being confident, and having an attitude of gratitude.

"Our attitude in life determines life's attitude toward us."

65

THRIVE

Live in the present. Focus on what you can do in the present moment. Don't worry about what you should have done last week or what you might be able to do tomorrow. The only time you can affect is the present. If you speculate too much about the past or the future, you won't get anything done. Tomorrow or next week frequently turns into never.

It takes courage to take action without instructions. Perhaps that's why initiative is a rare quality that's coveted in the business world. Seize the initiative. When you have a good idea, start implementing it without being told. Once people see you're serious about getting things done, they'll want to join in. The people at the top don't have anyone telling them what to do. If you want to join them, you should get used to acting independently.

Have you ever noticed that the most difficult part of public speaking is waiting for your turn to speak? Even professional speakers and actors experience pre-performance anxiety. Once they get started, the fear disappears. Action is the best cure for fear. The most difficult time to take action is the very first time. After the ball is rolling, you'll build confidence, and things will keep getting easier. That *confidence* breeds *momentum*, and you're then in high gear!

Go get 'em: Yesterday is history, tomorrow is not promised, but today is a gift...that's why they call it the *present*...

"Faith is taking the first step even when
you don't see the staircase."
— MARTIN LUTHER KING, JR.

66

CARPE DIEM

Don't wait until conditions are perfect. If you're waiting to start until conditions are perfect, you probably never will. There will always be something that isn't quite right. Either the timing is off, the market is down, or there's too much competition. In the real world, there is no perfect time to start. You have to take action and deal with problems as they arise. The best time to start was last year. The second best time is right now.

Go get 'em: If you want it enough, you can do it. Why not get started now?

"We learn to walk by stumbling."
— BULGARIAN PROVERB

67

RELEASE

Be a doer. Practice doing things rather than thinking about them. Do you want to start exercising? Do you have a great idea to pitch your boss? Do it today. The longer an idea sits in your head without being acted on, the weaker it becomes. After a few days the details get hazy. After a week it's forgotten completely. By becoming a doer, you'll get more done and stimulate new ideas in the process.

Remember that ideas alone don't bring success. Ideas are important, but they're only valuable after they've been implemented. One average idea that's been put into action is more valuable than a dozen brilliant ideas that you're saving for "some other day" or the "right opportunity." If you have an idea that you really believe in, do something about it. Unless you take action it will never go anywhere.

Go get 'em: Sometimes the best helping hand you can get is a good, firm push.

"The greatest thief this world ever produced is procrastination, and he is still at large."

68

TIME

What we do with this most precious of assets dictates our level of accomplishment, gratification, and ultimate peace of mind. There is nothing we can attain or strive for that remotely should be valued, with the exception of our close relationships, as we do our time and what we do with it. You can rationalize that you made money, accomplished all of your appointments, and "clocked in" every day; but living to the fullest is what sets you apart. This means appreciating things properly, honoring others, and respecting yourself and others. These traits should be inherent. Sometimes due to one's past or the lack of guidance, they're not. Remember though, they can still be learned and practiced every day.

Go get 'em: Decide what you want, decide what you are willing to exchange for it. Establish your priorities and get to work. You can have it.

"Worry more about your character than your reputation. Character is what you are, reputation merely what others think you are."
—JOHN WOODEN

69

THE ROAD TO PEACE OF MIND

It's up to you to get it done.

Do your homework, follow-through, and leave no stone un-turned. Communicate as clearly as you can!

Don't take things personally.

When you've done all you can, you've satisfied all that can be asked of you from the only one you truly must satisfy: *yourself!*

Always do your best.

This means ever-changing parameters, as you continue to grow and become more resourceful. What shouldn't change is integrity of effort. When this is present, you avoid three of the most destructive emotions possible: self-judgment, self-doubt, and regret!

Be impeccable with your word.

Make it clear and honest; you'll waste less time, get more done, and sleep better!

> "Reputation can't be manufactured…it must be earned…"

Keep your character above reproach; reputation will follow.

There's *nothing* more important. Anything else can be lost, and regained, but not always the case with your credibility and honor.

Pirket Avot: Jewish morality law.

In Jewish religion, there are 613 commandments put forth that it is said are instrumental to a *life well lived.* While one is hard-pressed to recite all these commandments, or laws, here are a few:

- To honor the old and the wise.
- Not to stand by idly when a human life is in danger.
- Not to lay down a stone for worship (no idols).
- Not to add to the commandments of the Torah.

The last one listed I feel gives a clear-cut synopsis of the Ten Commandments, the *Pirket Avot* (otherwise known as the Jewish morality law), and indeed, all we really need to know about how we should aspire to *always* conduct ourselves. This law follows:

The world is sustained by three things: by truth, *by* justice, *and by* peace. Put another way, as the prophet Hillel translated the laws and commandments that make up the Torah: "Treat others how you'd like to be treated...all the rest is commentary."

It means not *translating* the laws we live by in a manner convenient to us, but what is best for others.

What else must we need to know to conduct our lives in a manner that raises the calibration of the world around us and repairs the world in a way we can see as tangible? We can make excuses for our actions, rationalize to ourselves why we compromised our integrity for personal gain, or merely take the easy road. Whether anyone else ever knows, if we have proper self-respect, we will always remember. And self-respect is what comes from all the positives we lend to our lives, and not giving in to the negatives.

———————

Go get 'em: Today, make sure your positives outweigh your negatives.

"What you leave behind is not what is engraved in stone monuments, but what is woven into the lives of others."

70

PEACE OF MIND

Taking Pericles's words a step further, what is compiled in a lifetime isn't nearly as important as the impact left on others. You can affect positively—and profoundly—those around you, and indeed a small "universe" of people you don't even know… again, raising the calibration of the world.

Could there be truer words spoken? The oft-used adage: "When your time here is finished, will you find yourself saying: 'I should have spent that extra few hours at the office' or 'I wish I would have worked that one extra weekend'?" Probably not.

Go get 'em: There's not enough money in the world to buy peace of mind that lasts. It's what you give, in fact, not what you accumulate, that lays the foundation for it.

"Success is not to be pursued; it is to be attracted by the person you become."
— JIM ROHN

71

YOUR BEST VERSION OF YOU

Examples of positive "marks" left on the world are found in quiet acts of kindness toward others, especially those less privileged than yourself. One can never know the effect, even life-changing impact, a simple acknowledgment of someone can bring. Especially when you come from a point of credibility, be sure not to waste the respect you've garnered. By smiling or conversing with someone who sees you as proven, you raise their sense of pride by proliferating their belief in themselves.

Go get 'em: When you do something for someone else, especially one in need, notice how much more gratifying it is than going shopping (most of the time!). It also becomes a "self-fulfilling" prophecy; the more you do it, the more you want to.

"Every thought is a seed. If you plant crab apples, don't count on harvesting golden delicious."
—BILL MEYER

72

REPUTATION

My grandfather told me many times, and showed me by his actions, that you can have all the money in the world, but the greatest wealth lies in keeping your reputation spotless. He came to America from Damascus, Syria, and sold ties on the street, walking the streets of Dallas all day long, speaking very little English. He and my grandmother opened Freda Baby and Linen (her name was Freda), a small shop in Dallas, and never compiled much in the way of hard assets. However, they raised seven children and were greatly respected by the Jewish community in Dallas, moving to Tyler, Texas, in later life to live with my aunt, who cared for them to the end of their lives. Joining the synagogue in Tyler, my grandfather (Aaron J. Levy) became the patriarch of the Jewish community in no time and was most well known for blessing all the children (and every adult at some point) with the well-known "three-fold blessing":

> May the Lord bless you and keep you.
> May the Lord shine his countenance upon you
> and be gracious unto you.
> May the Lord show favor unto you and grant
> you peace.

A. J. Levy would sing to me in Arabic (the language they spoke to my mother, aunts, and uncles when they didn't want us to know what they were saying). As I put my head on his lap, I could feel his love for me, and in his persona could tell how much he appreciated being in America, how he honored his wife and family, and the respect he gave to his fellow man. His was a life well lived!

He treated others the way he would like to be treated. The rest of life, simply, is *commentary*.

Go get 'em: Keep your character pristine. Your reputation will follow close behind.

"Man never made any material as resilient as the human spirit."
—BERNARD WILLIAMS,
English philosopher

73

STUCK

Shenpa is the Tibetan term for attachment or being stuck. At the subtlest level, we feel a tightening, a tensing, a sense of closing down. Then we feel a sense of withdrawing, not wanting to be where we are. That's the hooked quality. That tight feeling has the power to draw us toward self-degradation, blame, anger, jealousy, and other emotions that lead to words and actions that end up hurting others, or ourselves.

One way to get past this urge to shut down is to realize the very impermanence we're uncomfortable with works as a positive, for the so-called failures we inevitably experience are fleeting, just as the "comfort zone" we used to always strive for. This is the perfect time to release.

It's okay not to be always "hitting on all cylinders." In fact, it's part of life, and necessary. Without this intermission of flow, we wouldn't appreciate when everything's working. We're only human, so relax.

Breathe; accept what's happening now. Know you will overcome this temporary state and find the resilience to continue striving. Each of these experiences conquered is like money in the bank confidence-wise. When we realize this and learn the true lessons here: determination, stick-to-itiveness, compassion toward others and ourselves—we become the masters of our destiny, no matter what experiences outside our control occur.

Practices to help us become "unstuck":

1) Write. A great way to revisit your aspirations, hopes, and dreams. Update to track your progress.
2) Think positive. When you do, you're halfway down the road

to fulfillment. Also, you can overcome or move through anything. Remember that.

3) Learn. Confidence, energy, and self-empowerment emerge when you keep energized with fresh knowledge.

4) Forgive. Holding grudges only hurts you. You take back control of your life when you forgive.

Go get 'em: If what's holding you back has to do with someone else, *forgive* them. You'll immediately gain "good" energy from taking charge of your feelings, and the momentum will have begun.

"When we have done our best, we should
wait the result in peace."
—J. LUBBOCK

74

VIRTUE

The Roman emperor Marcus Aurelius, who ruled from CE 161 to 180, adopted his philosophy as a young boy from the great Stoic teacher Epictetus. As a Stoic, Marcus believed that the only real goods worthy of pursuing are virtues. Wisdom, temperance, justice, courage…in effect, all things of a good moral character. All else he considered transient, cheap, and superfluous.

His willingness to take on as his chief mentor Epictetus, an ex-slave, seems confirmation of the true value he placed upon one's real soul, without regard to placement in society, even his own.

In my lifetime around our family business, a pawnshop, growing up working, watching, and learning how my parents conducted themselves with our customers, the greatest lesson I got from them was not how to size up a diamond, make a loan, or sell things. What has stuck with me all these years was their daily example of treating everyone with respect, no matter how little means they may have. The greatest feeling I get, and tribute to their "raising the calibration" of the world around them, is that customers from decades ago that I run into today tell me how a word, or deed, of my parents—or grandparents—in our store made a lasting impression. The funny thing is: our customers returned to us as much—in so many intangible ways—as we gave them.

Their examples of respect and sacrifice taught me that no matter your economic or social strata, inherent within a person and completely under that individual's control is the *dignity* with which they live. When I saw a customer whom I knew was struggling to support a family or who was out of work conduct themselves with more class than one with inherent entitlement, one is reminded of one of the lessons a *"life well lived"* is all about. When one understands the value of living a life with compassion, cares for others where the chance is there, and conducts themselves with dignity, they're indeed fortunate, and have more than the vast majority of those they encounter. From this, there usually follows enough to exist with.

Go get 'em: No matter what else you do, *lend yourself to someone* every day…

1) *help* someone
2) *impact* someone
3) *inspire* someone

"The strongest warriors are these two...time and patience."
— LEO TOLSTOY

75

GIVING BACK

From Aurelius:

> How small a fraction of infinite and unimaginable time has been assigned to each of us. For all too swiftly it vanishes in eternity. And what a fraction of the whole of matter, and what a fraction of the whole of universal soul. And on what a small clod of the whole earth you creep. Bearing all this in mind, imagine nothing to be great but this: to act as your own nature directs, and to love what universal nature brings. (*Meditations*, 12 32)

How did Aurelius find inner peace, after day upon day of shouldering his staggering duties as an imperial ruler? Equating to today's life, how do we find balance, and one step further, peace of mind?

He often in his philosophies, later compiled as a twelve-book compilation known as *Meditations,* could be found taking what many prize the most—wealth, power, luxuries, sex—stripping them of their glitz and glamour and revealing how truly empty they can be. He doesn't implore his people to disregard these aspects; chiefly, to keep them in perspective, as lesser elements to a life well lived:

> What else…than to do good to people, to bear with them and to show forbearance. (*Meditations*, 5 33)

Concern for tolerance of others and unity of the masses is a common theme he promoted, in an age where rulers often had little regard for their minions:

> Human beings are here for the sake of one another; either instruct them or put up with them. (*Meditations*, 8 59)

Go get 'em: Put to paper the things you value in life. Make sure they are worthy.

"Don't try to be perfect; just be an
excellent example of being human."
— ANTHONY ROBBINS

76

ALL YOU WANT

> Our security in life is to see each thing in itself,
> in its entirety, its material, its cause; and to do
> what is right and to speak the truth with all our
> heart. What remains but to enjoy life, linking
> one good act to another, so that not even the
> smallest space is ever left in between? (*Meditations*, 12 29)

Translated, I think Aurelius sees among the greatest virtues in
life complete honesty, both in our words and dealings with others, as well as our feelings, so as to be able to take in all of life,
just as it comes, and not with built-in expectation.

In a letter to his rhetoric teacher, Marcus Cornelius Fronto,
Aurelius reports that he is a lucky man because from Fronto he
learns "how to speak the truth; and that ability, to tell the truth,
is a hard task indeed, for men and gods alike." Is it any easier
for us today?

The busier our docket becomes, the more we think we need
to do fill our days, *acquire* things. In short, as we have opportunity to continually over-complicate our lives, this age-old message, fraught with simplicity, takes on added significance.

Go get 'em: Take all of life in. Every single day of it. As a quilt is
most noticeable when made up of an array of shapes, paths, and
designs, we are our best when we experience and offer the same.

"When I stand before God at the end of my life, I would hope that I would not have a single bit of talent left, and could say, 'I used everything you gave me.'"
—ERMA BOMBECK

77

LIFE WELL LIVED

I asked some pretty tough questions at the beginning of this book. I hope you have found some answers within these pages. It's not about what you accumulate in life, but those you touch and the mark on earth that you leave. When you own the ground you walk on, you breathe easier and fuller. Make sure the principles you live by are your own and of the highest caliber. That is something no one can erase, the imprint you leave.

Don't ever underestimate the difference you can make in one's life by an action, a response, even a simple smile. Notice how someone lights up when you don't just walk by in an office or on the street. Sadly, it's all too expected that we hurry by with no acknowledgment. Therefore, it's met with such joy when the opposite occurs. You literally change the world for the better with a simplistic gesture.

Take note of how much better *you* feel after making someone's day. If it's already a good day, you build upon your *momentum* and your mood is instantly enhanced. If you're having one of the days when nothing seems to add up, a small moment of kindness can do more for you than the person for whom the kindness was intended.

When you reach out to acknowledge someone who's really in need, you're not only extending a deed of kindness, you may be changing someone's life. This may sound like a drastic overstatement; it's not. By living your life with compassion, everyone around you is elevated. They relay those same traits to those they encounter, everything seems more positive, and life becomes more of a celebration!

I would like to close my thoughts with one of the most

dramatic and emotional moments of my life. It was a summer afternoon in 1972, and my father and I were at the pawnshop working it by ourselves. I was fourteen years old, no longer a boy, not quite a man. Although we had many nice people come through the door throughout the years, we also had our share of questionable characters. This particular afternoon was soon to play out as one of most dangerous days in our family's history.

My father was sitting at the counter, and I was sitting close by. We had been casually chatting, as the afternoon was rather slow that day. Only my father and I were working, as my grandmother had left, and my mother in this very hour was preparing to see my sister, Vikki, graduate from Columbia University and the Jewish Theological Seminary in New York City.

Almost ready to close for the night, suddenly the door flew open, and immediately we both sensed something was wrong— terribly wrong. It wasn't uncommon for someone to bring a gun into the pawnshop, but this was different. The nineteen-year-old man was screaming and yelling as he charged the store. As my father stood up, he tried to calm him, angling his attention away from me. When the young man saw movement, he shot my father. As my father went to the ground, the shooter stepped over my dad, and I remember thinking, *Don't shoot him again!*

In one moment, that young man changed our lives forever. I no longer felt safe and secure. I knew then that my father wasn't invincible. I realized that life could be over without any warning, and I understood for the first time that each moment counted. I was no longer a boy with a boy's problems. Having had my bar mitzvah a year previous, I was labeled in the Jewish religion a "man." I may not have felt like one then, but with my father shot and bleeding, it was my time to act as one.

As quickly as he entered the store, the felon left. Fortunately, the shot hit my father in the rear, and he wasn't killed. He yelled for me to lock the doors, and I tried my best to move swiftly, but my feet felt like lead. My heart was pounding, and I fumbled trying to get the keys to work. Time felt as though it had stopped, yet every second counted. I feared the man might return to finish us off so there would be no witnesses. My mind raced, but I had to stay on task and get the doors locked before I could process the thoughts flying around in my head and what to do next.

My father mustered what little strength he had, and his first thought was to protect me. He wanted to make sure we were safe. He struggled to his feet and helped me get the store closed up. By the amount of blood he lost, the fact he was in danger, despite his composure, was becoming clearer by the moment.

The ambulance soon arrived, and my father was taken to emergency surgery. In the darkest moment of my dad's life, his character was evident. He was thinking about me. His lifestyle was forever altered; my mind-set was forever changed.

We all "meet the republic," as was the description my grandfather gave it, at one time or another. This means responding to real world challenges, crises, and inevitable hardships…acting with a sense of responsibility and never losing sight of that. This is the last way I ever would have wished for it to happen, but a level of maturity was introduced into my life that day.

When these events occur, it's like a fork in the road—you can take either direction. Fortunately, the route bestowed upon me included an overriding view of optimism and a deep-seated trust that *right* prevails.

In the years that followed, my dad was able to swim and stay active, but he never ran much again. Maybe that makes me appreciate and love running even more. Maybe it makes me more determined not to give up running without a fight, for it is a gift that God has given me—the heart of an athlete. Thank you for that.

Dad, you're missed each day and always remembered. Yours was truly a life well lived.

Go get 'em: It's your time! Make it a truly "world-class" day, *athletes*!

ORDINARY HEROES

ORDINARY HEROES

ORDINARY HEROES

ORDINARY HEROES

YOU CHOOSE THE PATH:
Amy Palmiero-Winters

Amy Palmiero-Winters is a thirty-seven-year-old mother of two who works full time and is a coach, mentor, and below-the-knee amputee. As the result of a motorcycle accident in 1994 followed by 27 surgeries, Palmiero-Winters' leg was amputated below the knee. Prior to her accident, Amy ran competitively in a variety of events including the marathon. Following her amputation she quickly resumed this pursuit.

Amy currently holds world records in 12 different events within her division including the Ironman Triathlon, 100-mile Ultramarathon, and the 24-hour run, where she posted the second-fastest time in race history and became the first female amputee to finish a 100-mile race. In 2009, she won the female division at the 10th Annual Heartland "Spirit of the Prairie" 100-Mile Endurance Run. Based on this accomplishment, Amy was recognized by USA Track and Field as the athlete of the week in October. More recently, she was listed by the *Washington Times* as one of the top ten runners of the decade.

In January 2010, Amy qualified for the United States able-bodied twenty-four-hour run team that will be competing at the world championship in Brive, France, in May 2010, becoming the first amputee runner or athlete with a physical disability to compete against able-bodied counterparts on a world championship team. Amy's words, like her life, are inspirational:

> We all have two choices when faced with adversity: give up or be great...I had a strong foundation growing up as a child and, leg or not, nothing was going to stop me from reaching my dreams...At the age of eight I realized running was something I loved to do, and to this day it still holds true. I love to run and I am proud of who I have become because of running. Running has helped me through a lot of things in my life,

and I hope others will see in the same respect that we are all the same. We all have something that makes us happy and if we focus on that it can help us get through anything.

Amy's training entails some unusually altruistic features. In preparing for 24-hour able-bodied World Championships in June, a "normal" weekend might be for her to run a marathon, where she may be a featured speaker, lend inspiration and motivation, or simply have been invited to "raise the game" of the event for its participants. Amy doesn't race these events in most cases, though; she runs them *pushing* a young athlete from that city whom she's chosen, and when she does so, often she places a challenge before them as part of the "agreement."

At the Little Rock Marathon, early March 2010, eleven-year-old Ben, who has cerebral palsy, touched Amy in a way that made her want to accompany him through the finish line. Amy told me the day before the race that Ben's challenge would be to come up with three physical goals for himself by the time they reached the finish, and by the smiles they each had when they crossed the line, I'm confident Ben made good on his promise.

Here's a competitive elite marathoner who sacrifices her performance—and more of the spotlight—to give back, and raise the world's calibration in the process.

Aside from being a mother, athlete, mentor, and coach, Amy is a sports programs director for New York-based A Step Ahead Prosthetics. She is also the program director for ASPIRE, a non-profit organization.

Amy Palmeiro-Winters is a quintessential example that not only in athletics, but all walks of life, we're truly in control of our destiny.

[One week before the first printing of this book, in an exclusive ceremony at New York Athletic Club on April 14, 2010, the Amateur Athletic Union honored Amy Palmeiro-Winters with its highest honor, the James E. Sullivan Award. Presented annually for the past eighty years to the top amateur athlete in the country, the Sullivan Award is often called the "Oscar" of sports awards.]

A RUNNER'S WORLD:
Bart Yasso

Probably no person alive has run more road races in more exotic, meaningful locations than Bart Yasso, the chief running officer of *Runner's World* magazine. He's most recognizable as one of the great motivators and speakers on all that is positive about running, and has reawakened his marathoning career in his mid-50s.

What foremost impresses me about Bart is his tireless energy in pursuit of helping people be all they can be, and along the way lending inspiration to the mix. What he does far transcends the sport he loves. Whether running with the troops in Iraq or heading to all seven continents to run and speak, Bart urges the masses to challenge themselves in whatever arena they compete and be all they can be.

From Bart:

> As a breed, runners are a pretty gutsy bunch. We constantly push ourselves to discover limitations, then push past them. We want to know how fast we can go, how much pain we can endure, and how far our bodies can carry us before collapsing in exhaustion. But I urge you to take it a step further and test the boundaries of life, not just your physical prowess. You already know the rewards of putting one foot in front of the other. Sure, it's hard at first, but who hasn't looked back and wished they had done it sooner or been baffled that they were ever afraid or hesitant in the first place? Moving outward is an act of courage, and in my life, running has also been a vehicle of introduction to people, places, and cultures.

"LUCKY":
Dick Beardsley

No matter who you are, at sometime in your life you will have an obstacle or two that you will have to deal with. It could be an injury, a disappointment, a breakup; the list goes on and on. Don't ever forget, what may seem like not such a big deal to you, may be huge for someone else and visa versa! In the end, it is how you deal with that adversity that determines the type of person you are and the kind of life you will have!

Three things I've always kept in the forefront of my mind-good times and bad-have been at the core of why I never gave in to "breaks" in life, as dark as times looked at times:

1) Hard work
2) Positive spirit
3) Grace of God

I had a string of "bad" things happen in my life from the late 1980s to the mid 1990s, but as I look back, being able to deal with them in a positive way and getting through them has made me a much better more compassionate person today.

In 1989 I was involved in a very serious farm accident. I got wound up in a piece of farm machinery and had all the ribs on my right side broken, a punctured right lung, a broken right arm, a piece of steel driven into my chest, fractured vertebrae in my back, and my left leg was just about torn off. Twice the doctors thought they would have to amputate my left leg, some said I would never be able to walk again. I was ready to deal with that, but until I could find out for myself that I may not walk again, I was going to work real hard and keep a positive outlook, the best way I knew, by setting aside popular opinion—even from professionals—and quietly working to get better.

With the help of many people, a positive spirit, and the Grace of God, I recovered and eventually even got back to running again. It was but two years later and I was in a bad car accident when a lady ran a stop sign and T-boned my car. I had severe whiplash, a badly bruised spinal chord, and broken bones in my back. I had numerous surgeries and was very fortunate to completely recover. Again, I look back to the three things that got me through the farm accident, working hard in rehab, keeping the positive spirit going, and the Grace of God.

A year later I was running down a road and was hit by a truck, back in the hospital, more surgeries, but I survived. Six months later I was hiking with my son, the ground gave out, and I fell off a cliff! Back in the hospital, more surgeries, but again I survived, because of those three things, working hard in rehab, keeping the positive spirit going, and the Grace of God.

Friends would say to me, "Beardsley, if you didn't have bad luck, you wouldn't have any luck at all" I never believed that for a minute! The worst though was yet to come. I became addicted to narcotic painkillers. So many people told me it was not my fault; it was the doctors for giving me all the pills. I never once put the blame on anyone except myself. Thankfully I got through it by doing those three things, working hard in rehab, keeping the positive spirit going, and the Grace of God. I've now had over thirteen years of sobriety and have enjoyed every minute of it!

For all of us, life has its ups and downs, that is just part of living. Four things I try and do every morning when I awake have helped me tremendously over the years. Hopefully they can help you, too: "Every morning I try to wake with a smile on my face, enthusiasm in my voice, joy in my heart, and faith in my soul."

[*Dick Beardsley* burst into the worldwide running spotlight by creating one of the most electrifying marathon battles in history, the "Duel in the Sun" with Alberto Salazar at the Boston Marathon in 1982. After running virtually the entire race shoulder-to-shoulder, Dick was edged out by Alberto, with both breaking the American record in the distance.]

WELL LIVED:
Elora

This is a young lady who by her sheer aura had a profound effect upon me. When you first lay eyes upon her the happiness with which she lives is overriding and infectious. If you're having a so-called "rough" day and see Elora, you're instantly elevated and can feel—and see—outside just your own existence. Elora puts a smile on your face with her unbridled joy, and though I began as her "fitness coach," she's lent so much more to my life than I ever could to hers.

Did I mention Elora has cerebral palsy and spends the great majority of her time in a wheelchair? Probably not, as it's the last thing I ever think about when I see her. You see, Elora is filled with the joy that can't come from money, status or fame.

She lives with the gratitude you would expect from one who had been blessed with every luxury, privilege, and advantage this world offers. Instead, everything Elora does from a physical standpoint is effort-laden, and to leave her chair largely takes the help of someone else. Would you *ever* hear a complaint from her lips, or see a "poor me" facial expression? I haven't yet, and I've known her over five years.

Since that time (I met Elora when she was fifteen) all I've been greeted with is a reminder of the *best* that humanity has to offer. There's the interest she shows in everybody….a genuine concern for your welfare.

It takes great courage to release the familiar and seemingly secure, and embrace the new. This can translate as life altering when growth is the potential before you, as there's no real security in what is no longer meaningful. This is why we're here; there's life in movement, and in change there is great self-empowerment.

Elora welcomes new goals into her life constantly, with independence always at the forefront of her pursuit. She doesn't complain; just wants every chance to make the most of her life wherever possible. A lot of us are hamstrung from time to time by letting difficulties draw our focus away from the elements that can "raise our game," making hazy both our goals and our effort. I marvel how I don't see that in Elora. Frustration at times, yes. A desire to "throw in the towel," never!

Elora's nature of kindness is equaled by her continual striving to be all she can be. Elora is in constant pursuit—despite her physical shortcomings—of a way to better herself. It's heartwarming and truly inspiring to witness, and I'm better for being able to be there to see her rise above the circumstances, day in and day out.

From doing whatever it takes to make herself more mobile, like learning to operate new wheelchairs, she breaks away from the familiar with not only desire but zest. At the first printing of this book, Elora was a sophomore in college, on a two-year plan to live independently.

THE YOUNG RUNNERS:
Jim and Shirley Hoke

This is a couple I've known now for five years, and one that makes it crystal clear we're only limited by "self-imposed" restrictions. These "80-something young folks" are memorable as individuals, and unforgettable as a couple.

Shirley has run the Marathon Du Medoc in Bourdeaux, France, twice in the past five years, and she continues to pursue fitness and personal growth in a manner most half her age wouldn't aspire to. She's a voracious reader of impressively diverse subject matter, and her demure nature is a noticeably beautiful addition anywhere she goes. Most noticeable with Shirley is that her interests and desire to learn and experience things hasn't been dwarfed by popular opinion of how we should conduct ourselves in our "golden" years. Shirley is a pilot, marathoner, and writes letters still. Her penmanship is unique to her and etched with dignity that is all Shirley Hoke. Receiving something written by her, you know exactly from whom it came. She finds ways to give gifts with that personal touch that shines through clearly in all her endeavors. Shirley Hoke is understated, yet always noticeable.

Jim Hoke, Shirley's husband of sixty years, on the other hand, will speak to anyone and everyone. And better than that, he'll listen to everybody. Jim is the most well-rounded, accomplished person in the room, and he measures *success* the right way!

Jim took up running about thirty years ago, when approaching fifty, and one can find him cheering Shirley on in races around the country, at which they appear sometimes on a whim. He'll run them, too. I began coaching the Hokes (I contend they've always "coached" me in this relationship) five years ago, as they wanted to become stronger, faster runners. They taught me something from Day 1.

I explained that from my viewpoint they were doing great, as running consistently through your upper-70s by most standards is "over the top" as a pursuit. These folks are not most people, and you know it when around Jim. He asks your opinion and questions about yourself—whether he's known you a lifetime, or you just met—and it's literally hard to find out all he's done, accomplished and the footprint he's left on this world. When in the presence of such a person, and usually they're older, more understated than ostentatious in their mannerisms, it's important to know it. Glean what you can from the experience. If you're lucky enough to become close to them, savor the time, even if you think it'll come around again soon.

Finally, if they seek you out, don't take this blessing for granted. Maybe you're doing something right! No need to focus on that though; whether or not it's the case, be assured you're the fortunate one in the equation. The Hokes have taught me grace, humbleness, and the importance of listening to all around me. Be discerning, but don't discount prematurely, either due to appearance or perceived placement in society. Jim and Shirley continue to instill how vital it is to keep one's own understatedness in life intact. Not to deny or denigrate your accomplishments, but as importantly, not to wear them on your sleeve!

NO EXCUSES:
Richard Vaughn

As a junior high school athlete in the late 1960s I ran cross country in track. As I moved into high school, my attention turned to basketball. Looking back, for all intents and purposes, I must have assumed my running "career" was done. I managed to letter in basketball and even went to the state tournament in my senior year, where we fell a few points short of a state championship. Then, it was off to college and a potential basketball scholarship. Or so I thought.

At the age of seventeen and shortly after graduation, a severe accident—a fall of roughly eighty-five feet from a scaffolding—left me paralyzed and in a wheelchair. This was in the early 1970s. As there were few truly organized wheelchair sports available anywhere, and absolutely none in small town USA, I was completely sedentary and not terribly far from losing hope for the first time in my life.

In 1978, at the age of twenty-five, I met four other people who were in wheelchairs. We formed a local wheelchair basketball team, which shortly became one of the elite teams in America. We won five National Championships in the 90s, with the last one coming in 2000.

Having been relegated to wheelchair sports as a means of staying physically fit since I was in my early twenties, I have tried to apply myself as though I was playing in the NBA for the World Championship. I'd like to think this is because, although the sports I participate in are adapted to the disabled, I don't really see my life *or* my adaptation as being any more difficult than what other people face in their particular lives. After all, each of us has our own unique challenges. Most of us, well, adapt.

After a long and personally rewarding twenty-five years of playing wheelchair basketball, I began to realize that age was working against me. The sport of basketball truly is for the young. On a dare, I turned to marathons as a mid-life outlet for my energies, as well as a means of staying healthy for as long as possible.

It boggles the mind to imagine how many "pushes" it took to get up and down a basketball court for twenty plus games a year over twenty-five years. By the same token, the thought of pushing a wheelchair 26.2 miles in one day was nearly beyond imagination. However, not being one to turn down a challenge, my mind was made up.

The first night I took my standard, rigid-frame basketball wheelchair out on the streets was, to say the least, an adventure. A hill! I took it. Another hill! I took it. Soon, my wife was calling me on my cell phone that night in 2005. "Are you OK, Richard?" "Never better!" But then I realized I was cold and probably should head home. Out of curiosity, we took the car out later that night and measured the course I had followed—nine miles. I was hooked.

The first marathon, the very hilly LR race, took a long time; five hours, I think. But the sport, marathoning, was far and away greater than anything I had ever done. It was the camaraderie, the challenging hills, the rough roads and, finally, the finish line, and more camaraderie.

There is one more thing I can add about camaraderie. During the race, people would pass me (or I them) and say, "You are quite an inspiration." But that works both ways in that it inspires me. After all, when someone calls you an inspiration, what are you going to do, quit?! The point is, by being called an inspiration, I was equally inspired to finish the race. This is further testimony to the social aspect of this sport.

I "ran" one more race that year...and hurt myself. Though completely unpreventable, the how isn't as important as the what, a cracked vertebrae in my neck. Following neck surgery that January, I didn't race at all in 2006. The surgeon said I probably should find something else to do. Maudlin as it sounds, you may as well have taken away my best friend.

By May, I was back on the road, with my doctor's permission, of course. The following March, 2007, my life took another significant turn. After preparing for what I hoped would be the defining race of my life and going for my third finisher's medal, I met a fellow marathoner at the Little Rock Marathon Exposition. He had a booth and was recruiting runners for his own state's marathon.

I should add here that all of my races, 12 marathons (and counting) and several dozen 5K and 10K races have been done in a standard, 4-wheel chair. I do not use a three-wheeled racing chair or a cycle-propelled device. I had done one 5K race in a racing chair and it was not physically beneficial. I don't disparage those who use special chairs. In fact, I applaud everyone who participates. However, I had been racing for two specific purposes.

First, I raced to stay healthy. The very fact that my clunky, 26-lb chair is so difficult to push is also what keeps me physically fit. The light, 4-lb racing chairs take little effort to push and do not provide for me the results I need.

Second, I raced because it is a social sport. Except for the professional or semi-professional sprinters who race year round and in elite events, most people who participate have no illusions of "winning." On the other hand, anyone who crosses the finish line is a winner, in my mind. To that end, I preferred to run with the crowds, not away from them.

I digressed to these points because as I do run a rather unique style, the 4-wheel chair, I am invited to attend marathons in many different cities. Of course, no one can participate in the dozens of marathons held across the country each year. I was looking for events that might lead to the Boston Marathon or one just as prestigious.

Back to the "defining moment" I mentioned earlier. At the 2007 LR Expo, I stopped by a booth and talked to a person who would ultimately alter my attitude and change my outlook on racing forever. His name is Mark Bravo and he was "pitching" the Oklahoma City Marathon.

I visited with him for a few minutes and politely took a brochure. My parting thought as I dutifully deposited the brochure in my grab bag was, "What's in Oklahoma City that I couldn't find somewhere else?"

When I got home and was going through all my handouts, I spotted the OKC brochure. My heart nearly melted when I realized it was for the Oklahoma City Memorial, the F. Murrah Federal Building bombing of 1995 and the worst terrorist act on American soil by Americans, against Americans.

Two days after the bombing, I wrote down my own thoughts about this senseless act and presented it to my church. I had titled it, "Let the Healing Begin." This act, this tragedy, had been a sobering reality for me. Even though it touched my soul and led me to what I said, I couldn't fathom the effect it had on the citizens and affected families in Oklahoma City.

Further, while visiting OKC in 2002 on a business trip, I stayed in a hotel a few short blocks from the Memorial, which I made a point to tour. I can't describe the feelings I had as I left the Memorial.

Needless to say, I knew I had to run this race and immediately went online to sign up. This, despite the fact the OKC Marathon was only four weeks after the LR Marathon. I didn't know if I would have enough recovery time between the races to put on a decent showing in the OKC race. Truth to tell, I didn't care! I knew I would do my best to prepare and run the best race I could. But this was an event I would run. There would be no excuse.

I got in touch with Mark and apologized if I had been abrupt with him at the Expo. As well, I wanted to be sure the OKC route would accommodate wheelchair participants. The defining moment was that not only did I make an instant, lifelong friend, I found reason #3 to race. I would never again run a race that wasn't for a worthy cause.

What I gained was even greater. In one short race (if you can call 26.2 miles short) Oklahoma City in general and Mark Bravo in particular took me into their hearts, and I knew I would put this race on my calendar for as long as I was able to race, and put Mark Bravo's name in my Rolodex!

As an added bonus, in each of the three OKC Marathons I

have run, I've been allowed to put the name of one or more of the victims of the bombing on the back of my chair and run in memory of them. At the end of the race, I go back to the Memorial, find the person's memory seat, have my picture taken by it and email it to the family of the victim. This is a very special thing for me.

To sum this all up, I do race "the hard way." I do so for the reasons I spelled out. I also race for specific and worthy causes. And, in four racing years, I have met approximately 200,000 people I would not have otherwise met, none any more important than my friend, Mark Bravo. Also, I have yet to find any greater hospitality than I have found in the great State of Oklahoma, and specifically Oklahoma City.

Moving on, people ask me why I race. The short answer is because I want to live. The four guys in the wheelchairs who helped me form the wheelchair basketball team? None of them stayed with the program past the first few years. Sadly, none of them are still alive. The average life expectancy of a teenage paraplegic is 50 years. My friends went sedentary and are no longer alive. I, on the other hand, am nearly 58 and will race in my 13th marathon March 7, 2010. (And, Lord willing, my 14th the following month in OKC!)

People also ask me if I get tired during a race. Again, there is a short answer. With proper preparation, one can finish a marathon with relative ease. The longer answer, at least for me is, there have been many times I have felt I was too tired to push my chair. But I have not yet been too tired to push myself. I pray I maintain the wisdom to never push myself too far.

Thus far, that hasn't been a problem. The day I wrote this, my blood pressure was 117/74, with a pulse rate of 58. My BMI is 25.2 and my health makes a hero of my neurosurgeon. (That is barely a joke.)

Allow me to close with an ironic summation regarding this rather long story. As a teen, I began athletics with running and gave it up for basketball. As an adult, I gave up basketball for running. Wheelchair notwithstanding, the circle is complete.

DREAMER:

Pam Boteler

Realize the Dream – 2016 Olympic Inclusion for Women's Canoe
Written by Pam Boteler

What does this have to do with momentum? This title started with two key words: realize (a verb) and dream (a noun). We also have a date set (2016). A big part of living an extraordinary life is creating extraordinary goals, and taking actions to realize those goals. It's the taking action part, and being very clear about what you want, that can help create and build momentum, in any area of your life.

> "So many of our dreams at first seem impossible,
> then they seem improbable, and then, when we
> summon the will, they soon become inevitable."
> — CHRISTOPHER REEVE

For me personally, it is my mission, as an athlete and a lobbyist, to gain gender equity (equal events for women as the men) in one of the oldest summer Olympic sports—canoe/kayak—by 2016. This is the *last* summer Olympic sport to not have gender equity.

Sprint (or high kneel) canoe became an Olympic event in 1936; slalom canoe in 1972. But this is still a men's only club—dominated by antiquated thinking about women's abilities in sport, and the effects of participation on our bodies. Women have been prohibited from getting into these boats in countries around the world for decades. Even if they did occasionally paddle Olympic-style boats, it was usually with a man in a two-person canoe (because we could not possibly paddle them ourselves) and only for fun. In the U.S. women were barred from competing at the national championships until 2000, when they were permitted to race—against the men. Yes, in the U.S., after almost eighty years, we finally changed the national sport by-laws to recognize and include women. It was not until 2007 that the International Canoe Federation (ICF) officially "recognized" women's canoe and added the word "gender" to its anti-discrimination laws. Now in 2010, the ICF is including one event as official (earning medals) at the World Championships. And they included women's canoe for the first time ever in the 2010 World Cup events.

We have had two major barriers to inclusion: the first is the chicken and the egg syndrome, i.e., the ICF says "show us the athletes, we'll show you the events." We know that athletes will not come and countries and coaches will not support this without events. The second is the 100-year-old myth that racing high-kneel style in canoes will damage the female reproductive organs, causing infertility, and will cause lopsided development of the breasts. These people conveniently forget about men's cycling as a risk sport for men, and forget that women's reproductive organs are tucked away safely inside of us. For the first barrier, knowing this has made us work harder off the water, lobbying the ICF and national federations around the world and using the power of the internet to connect women around the world who are alone. For the 100-year-old myth, at first it made us angry to hear this and it was becoming more of a cancer than a driver. We thought the myth was dead by 2008, but in 2010, national federations expressed concern once again. But this time, we are using this to our advantage, viewing it as evidence of our momentum. Some people and cultures are still frightened of the power of women to choose what they want to do and our drive to get what we want. What we want them to realize is that we are here to *grow* the sport – and perhaps save this sport from extinction.

Building upon the success of the 2009 Worlds, and the announcements of the 2010 events and development camps, we are seeing an exponential increase in interest from numerous countries around the world, where we never thought possible. Particularly European countries, which have a stronghold on this sport as a "man's sport."

We are feeling the momentum as we connect with women

around the world via the internet and we get photos and videos from more and more countries. This becomes evidence to present to the ICF and to the Olympic Committee that this is real. Open the doors and women warriors of the single blade will paddle through. It takes only one brave soul in any country to do what was done in Canada and the U.S. 10-15 years ago.

We have a goal of 20 countries competing at the 2010 World Championships for both sprint and slalom and we feel we will reach this goal. Our momentum is building faster and faster because we have a clear vision and unwavering belief in what is possible—and what is right.

Being very clear about what you want in life and having the patience and determination to persevere through obstacles and setbacks are what create momentum for an extraordinary life, achieving extraordinary results, and realizing your wildest dreams.

> "Never doubt that a small group of thoughtful, committed citizens can change the world. Indeed, it is the only thing that ever has."
> — MARGARET MEAD (1901-1978)

[*Pam Boteler* is president of USA WomenCAN, and is a driving force in the global campaign for gender equity in Olympic canoeing. Boteler was the first woman in the U.S. to compete at the national championships in sprint canoe (and win gold) in 2000, against the men. At 41, Boteler continues to compete internationally and holds American records in several events. For more information visit: www.justcanoeit.com]

———————

AFTER THE MEDAL:
Joan Benoit Samuelson

Most known for winning the first Women's Olympic Gold Medal (Los Angeles, 1984) Joan Benoit Samuelson, at fifty-one, is still the quintessential figure in bringing women's distance running toward a par with the men. She continues to do so by leading the pack with performances that continue to crack the record books. Participating in the US Olympic Marathon Trials at age fifty was yet another of her groundbreaking performances.

Diminutive and modest, there is, however, no understatement in the passion she exudes, for everything she does. Joanie exudes care with everything she does. She's a master gardener and speaks around the country, promoting running, and furthering self-esteem for all, primarily children and women.

You wouldn't know, and she won't be the one to tell you, of her literally unprecedented accomplishments in running, and without bringing attention to herself she continues to test limits with her physical accomplishments and giving back (albeit quietly) to her community and society in general.

Every year she helps organize the Beach to Beacon 10-K, a world-class event she founded in her hometown, Cape Elizabeth. The race directs $30,000 annually to Maine nonprofit organizations that work with children.

When I came to know Joanie in 2007 at the Oklahoma City Memorial Marathon, I was a few days away from a hip replacement surgery. I thought I would introduce her to speak a few times that weekend, and that would be it. Knowing how reserved she is, I planned not to intrude upon that.

The hip procedure came up as we talked about our city, the bombing that led to creation of the race, and my past, as Joanie was generally interested in all those things. When I told her that the hip procedure was imminent in days, she not only wished me well, but continued to check on me after surgery. When she returned in 2009, she met my wife-to-be Leslie, and on the eve of our wedding she sent wonderful "wishes" our way. Bottom line: Joanie *cares* when she lends herself to something, and you can't fake that.

Whether it be by running or with her words of encouragement to all, Joanie has transcended her sport, and while it's still integral to her, running is more of a metaphor for her life than anything. She found what she could do well, nurtured her craft, and it became a springboard for her life to come. This Olympic Gold Medalist continues to stimulate her curiosity. She's climbed Mount Kilimanjaro, continues to train diligently, and explores new horizons in all aspects of her life.

"I used to plan my day around my running," she says. "Now I plan my running around my day."

[*Joan Benoit-Samuelson* won the first Olympic women's marathon in the 1984 Summer Olympics in a time of 2:24.52 in hot and smoggy conditions, more than a minute ahead of her rivals. This effort came despite arthroscopic surgery on her knee 17 days before the trials earlier that year. The athletes behind her were Grete Waitz, Rosa Mota and Ingrid Kristiansen, all marathon legends in their own right. She is a multiple-time Boston Marathon winner, with her 1983 course record standing for 11 years. Joanie continues to establish age-group records at various distances.]